CRAYONS AND iPADS

SAGE SWIFTS

In 1976 SAGE published a series of short 'university papers', which led to the publication of the QASS series (or the 'little green books' as they became known to researchers). Almost 40 years since the release of the first 'little green book', SAGE is delighted to offer a new series of swift, short and topical pieces in the ever-growing digital environment.

SAGE *Swifts* offer authors a new channel for academic research with the freedom to deliver work outside the conventional length of journal articles. The series aims to give authors speedy access to academic audiences through digital first publication, space to explore ideas thoroughly, yet at a length which can be readily digested, and the quality stamp and reassurance of peer-review.

CRAYONS AND iPADS

LEARNING AND TEACHING OF YOUNG CHILDREN IN THE DIGITAL WORLD

DEBRA HARWOOD

Los Angeles | London | New Delhi
Singapore | Washington DC | Melbourne

Los Angeles | London | New Delhi
Singapore | Washington DC | Melbourne

SAGE Publications Ltd
1 Oliver's Yard
55 City Road
London EC1Y 1SP

SAGE Publications Inc.
2455 Teller Road
Thousand Oaks, California 91320

SAGE Publications India Pvt Ltd
B 1/I 1 Mohan Cooperative Industrial Area
Mathura Road
New Delhi 110 044

SAGE Publications Asia-Pacific Pte Ltd
3 Church Street
#10-04 Samsung Hub
Singapore 049483

© Author and contributors 2017

First published 2017

Apart from any fair dealing for the purposes of research or private study, or criticism or review, as permitted under the Copyright, Designs and Patents Act, 1988, this publication may be reproduced, stored or transmitted in any form, or by any means, only with the prior permission in writing of the publishers, or in the case of reprographic reproduction, in accordance with the terms of licences issued by the Copyright Licensing Agency. Enquiries concerning reproduction outside those terms should be sent to the publishers.

Library of Congress Control Number: 2017936060

British Library Cataloguing in Publication data

A catalogue record for this book is available from the British Library

Editor: Natalie Aguilera
Assistant editor: Delayna Spencer
Production editor: Vanessa Harwood
Marketing manager: Susheel Gokarakonda
Cover design: Jen Crisp
Typeset by: C&M Digitals (P) Ltd, Chennai, India
Printed in the UK

ISBN 978-1-4739-1599-2
eISBN 978-1-4739-2712-4

At SAGE we take sustainability seriously. Most of our products are printed in the UK using FSC papers and boards. When we print overseas we ensure sustainable papers are used as measured by the PREPS grading system. We undertake an annual audit to monitor our sustainability.

CONTENTS

NOTES ON THE AUTHORS

Debra Harwood is an Associate Professor in the Faculty of Education at the Brock University, specializing in curriculum and pedagogy in early childhood education and care. She led the team of researchers on the Crayons and iPads project that examined children's thinking, interactions and ways of being within iPad-infused early childhood education classrooms.

Dane Marco Di Cesare serves as the Program Coordinator and Data Manager of the New York State Technical Assistance Center, as well as a lecturer at the Brock University. He has conducted a variety of research activities related to tablet use, multimodality and literacy with students of varying exceptionalities across different grade levels.

Kristy Fitzpatrick is an early childhood educator at the University of New Brunswick (UNB) Early Childhood Centre. She graduated from UNB with a specialization in early literacy in 2007. A photographer and a mother of two young boys, she aims to capture children's emotions, spiritedness and sense of wonder through her work.

Arlene Grierson is an Associate Professor at Nipissing University's Schulich School of Education where she teaches courses in Language Arts and Literacy. Her research explores the use of digital technologies and the impact of models of professional learning on teachers' growth and their students' literacy learning.

Andrew Hashey is an Assistant Professor in the Exceptional Education Department at SUNY College at Old Westbury. In his research, he explores technology integration to support literacy learning and teaching, self-regulated strategy development, Universal Design for Learning, and new literacies.

Tara Kaczorowski is an Assistant Professor in the Special Education Department at the Illinois State University. One of her methodology strengths is utilizing multimodal mixed-methods research involving video coding. Tara's primary research areas are special education teacher preparation and math instructional interventions for students with high-incidence disabilities.

Laura Lane is a PhD candidate in the Faculty of Education at the Brock University. Her research interests include forms of capital and privileged culture in university institutions, gender discourses in popular and digital media, educational possibilities of social media, technology in early-years classrooms, and discussion groups as sites for gender critique.

Leslie Memme has 22 years of teaching experience in early years and primary education. She has embraced the use of technology in the classroom throughout her career. Leslie is completing her Masters in Education at the Brock University with a focus on the use of iPads in classrooms.

Candace Mersereau received her BEd (Early Years) and MEd (Exceptional Learners) from the University of New Brunswick where she currently works as an early childhood educator in the University's Early Childhood Centre. She strives to support and cultivate children's confidence as learners through respectful listening, meaningful conversations, and with the provision of diverse learning opportunities.

Sherry Rose is a Co-Director of the Early Childhood Centre at the University of New Brunswick where she teaches in the areas of assessment, literacies and curriculum.

Jennifer Rowsell is Professor and Canada Research Chair in Multiliteracies at the Faculty of Education in Brock University where she directs the Centre for Multiliteracies. Her most recent books include the *Routledge Handbook of Literacy Studies* (2015) with Kate Pahl and *Literacy Lives in Transcultural Times* (2016) with Rahat Naqvi.

Katelyn Scott is a certified teacher and currently completing the master's program at the Brock University. As a research assistant, Katelyn has been involved in several projects related to iPad integration within early educational contexts.

Pam Whitty is an educator-researcher at the University of New Brunswick, working in early childhood studies, literacies and curriculum from a critical reconceptualist perspective. She has co-led provincial research-based early childhood curriculum and community-based literacy initiatives in New Brunswick. In 2015–16, she was co-chair of the New Brunswick Child Care Task Force Commission.

Kari-Lynn Winters is an Associate Professor at the Brock University. Her research interests include exploring multimodal literacies across a range of diverse contexts, drama in education, children's literature, and authorship as social, semiotic and critical assemblage. Her most recent book is *Youth, Critical Literacies, and Civic Engagement: Arts, Media, and Literacy in the Lives of Adolescents* (2015) with Theresa Rogers, Mia Perry and Ann-Marie LaMonde.

Vera E. Woloshyn is in the Faculty of Education at the Brock University. Her research and publication interests include working with children and young adults enrolled in postsecondary settings who experience learning challenges, exploring the role of iPads and other technologies in literacy instruction, and the use of popular culture as a learning tool.

ACKNOWLEDGEMENTS

On behalf of my contributing authors, I would like to take this opportunity to thank the children, educators, parents and administrators who took part in the research studies discussed throughout this book. Without their generosity in opening up their classrooms and lives to us and sharing their many stories, this book would not have been possible. I would also like to thank my colleague and friend Michelle Tannock who undertook reading an early draft of the manuscript and her willingness to provide feedback.

In addition, I would like to thank the funder of the research project that inspired the name of the book, *Crayons and iPads*. Social Sciences and Humanities Research Council of Canada provided generous support for this research project.

THE DIGITAL WORLD OF YOUNG CHILDREN

Debra Harwood

PERVASIVENESS OF TECHNOLOGY

Digital technologies are prevalent within western society, with 'smart' mobile use among young children escalating (e.g., tablets, iPads, smartphones). The anywhere/anytime access to the Internet, the convenient size and portability and relative inexpensiveness of smart mobile technologies make these devices extremely attractive within educational contexts. A recent report by Ofcom (2013) in the United Kingdom reported 'use of a tablet computer at home had tripled among 5–15s since 2012 (42% versus 14%) while one-quarter (28%) of 3–4s use a tablet computer at home' (p. 5). In addition, tablet computers are widely used in many educational classrooms, with rates reported as high as 70% among primary and secondary schools in the United Kingdom (Coughlan, 2014) and more than half of American early childhood educators having access to tablets in the classroom (a twofold increase since 2012) (Blackwell, Wartella, Lauricella & Robb, 2015). In Canada, a similar pattern has emerged with universal access to the Internet through portable devices by children 9–16 years of age (MediaSmarts, 2014). Seemingly, young children's play activities are impacted by this greater use of and access to mobile devices (e.g., streaming videos to tablets) (Edwards, 2013a; Moses, 2012). Attendant with this prevalence are the 'cautionary' tales of the potential negative impact of technology on young children. When writing this introduction, a quick Internet search revealed several featured articles that included concerns related to the unsafe nature of iPads (throughout the book, we will use the terms iPads and tablet interchangeably) and an emphasis on the detrimental effects of tablets on child development.

Yet, as Wohlwend (2010) explains, digital worlds are pervasive in young children's lives, and many 0–6-year-olds use media on a given day to read a book or listen to music. And toddlers and preschool-aged children do not appear to be passive media users; rather they actively engage in playing sophisticated games on cellphones, creating avatars, requesting and loading specific websites on the Internet (Rideout, Vandewater & Wartella, 2003). Thus far, the most widely cited research regarding the use of such devices in the home environment reveals a balanced approach (Plowman, McPake & Stephen, 2008, 2010; Stephen, Stevenson & Adey, 2013). Thus, despite the cautions, digital mediums are a part of the sociocultural context of young children's lives. Perhaps, as adults, we have yet to fully understand young children as 'emergent users of new literacies and new technologies' (Wohlwend, p. 144); thus, our somewhat technophobic notions persist.

In this book, I propose that understanding the young child's digital world is an important referent for educators (and adults in general). As such, I invited authors to contribute notions that would challenge traditional views of play and early childhood education (ECE; we have defined the term 'early childhood education' to refer to both school-based and community-located educational and care programs for children aged 3–8 years). Collectively, my fellow authors and I posit that technology – iPads specifically – provides an accessible and additional learning and instructional medium that can be used to provoke, ignite and excite children's interest in and exploration of the world around them. Ultimately, it is through this exploration and engagement that new discoveries are made and learning unfolds. As young children inquire about the world around them and their place in it, new and interesting ways to play and learn can emerge with iPads. For many of us contributing to this book, we were drawn to iPads and the worlds of children. The iPad, a relatively new digital medium within the ECE classrooms we were affiliated with, offered an exciting window to explore children's experiences and lived realities while also engaging all of us in questioning some of the taken-for-granted notions about early learning.

Many of our discussions throughout the book are allied with references to the various research studies we have engaged in as scholars. The book's title, *Crayons and iPads*, was inspired by one such study. Several of the contributing authors participated in this particular study and we jointly spent 10 months observing and documenting children's thinking and interactions before and after the research team introduced iPads within five different ECE classrooms. A full description of this study is available elsewhere (Harwood, 2014; Harwood et al., 2015). Here, we simply use vignettes from this study (and others) as provocations, common threads throughout the book and a starting point upon which to question notions of play, iPad-infused learning and teaching pursuits, and theoretical concepts within ECE.

NOTIONS OF PLAY IN THE 21ST CENTURY

What is play? Play is an elusive concept to define (Sutton-Smith, 1997). In the most general sense, play can be thought of as the antithesis of work. And although play might be easily recognizable, an irrefutable definition does not exist (Johnson, Christie & Yawkey, 1999). Mayfield (2001) provides one of the most comprehensive lists of the characteristics of play compiled from the work of researchers of the 20th century. She concludes that play is characterized by: the voluntary nature (child choice) of the activity, its meaningfulness, active engagement, intrinsic motivation, pleasure and enjoyment, non-literalness, child-directedness, naturalness, flexibility, spontaneity, freedom from adult rules, and enjoyment (p. 257). With the onset of the digital world and the pervasiveness of digital mediums in young children's lives, everything would now seem to have an online presence (Lim & Clark, 2010); thus, the nature of play appears to have somewhat shifted. Whether or not this 20th-century definition of play still holds true is unclear. However, if play is construed as a powerful social practice shaping children's immediate worlds (Wohlwend, 2014), the definition of play can be capacious and more encompassing of actual play worlds and behaviours of the 21st-century child.

Karen Wohlwend (2011) describes play as a tactic – a behaviour that 'manipulates the constraints in here-and-now reality to make alternative realities possible [enabling] children to create diversions and escapes while remaining in the same physical space' (p. 116). As children play, they participate and enter imagined spaces, 'communities to which they belong and hope to belong' (Kendrick, 2005, p. 9). In this manner, play is a conduit for identity-making (Holland, Lachicotte, Skinner & Cain, 1998) as well as a literary and social text (Kendrick). Kendrick's use of Schwartzman's (1976) metaphor of a 'sideways glance' of one child's dramatic play experience helps illustrate the diverse range of 'social, cultural, and textual' platforms that children draw from within their play frames (p. 6).

In the 21st century, these communities of play do include virtual and technological devices – a rhizomatic meaning-making space that involves both material/immaterial relationships (Burnett, Merchant, Pahl & Rowsell, 2014). Several of the chapters in the book also describe this convergence of 21st-century play (Edwards, 2013b). Likewise, I have previously discussed this melding of children's concrete play with digital play enabling young learners 'to enact new understandings, and engage in innovative meaning-making processes' (Harwood, 2014, p. 4). Importantly, the incorporation of children's perspectives and experiences within the definition of play is vital. Clearly, children view and enact the *appropriation, accommodation, assimilation* and/or *adaptation* (Marsh & Bishop, 2014) of digital worlds as important modes for their online/offline play contexts (Marsh, 2011). And given the haptic and moveable nature of the iPad, the seamlessness of online/ offline play, digital play is embodied play.

iPad-INFUSED INQUIRY PURSUITS

As a starting point, this book has adopted a converged (Edwards, 2013b) or hybrid view of play (Marsh, 2010) where children seamlessly blur their digital and non-digital activities (Plowman et al., 2010; Plowman, Stevenson, Stephen & McPake, 2012). By doing so, we draw attention to the potential of iPads in offering new avenues for exploring, experimenting and meaning-making (Yelland, 2011). Thus, the repertoire of experiences available within the 21st-century ECE classroom ought to include digital modes. Purposefully, as educators and scholars, we position our discussion alongside inquiry-based learning/pedagogies. As opposed to traditional pedagogies, the practice of inquiry is a spiral process that begins with the 'curiosity of the learner' (Bruce & Casey, 2012, p. 193) and invites exploration, experimentation, experiencing, problem-solving, analysis, collaboration, constructing and communicating new understandings (Bruce & Bishop, 2002; Bruce & Casey, 2012; Chiarotto, 2011). Like other researchers (Wang, Kinzie, McGuire & Pan, 2010), several of us have discussed elsewhere this fusion of iPads and inquiry (Harwood et al., 2015). Here, we again revisit this thinking and underscore iPads as an invitational space, an 'affinity space' (borrowing Gee's 2004 concept) – a classroom context where children engage in socio-critical negotiations that are at times collaborative while also fluid and discursive (Winters & Memme, this volume). Thus, the iPad, a 'placed resource' (Prinsloo, 2005) that is contextually relevant for young children, acts as a provocation and an important milieu for children's play and learning.

THEORETICAL MUSINGS

Several chapters within provide an in-depth discussion of the theoretical rationales underpinning the book. Here, I will simply outline our collective theoretical musings to help position the reader. Rowsell, in this volume, begins this thought process by underscoring how materialism/post-humanism, multimodality and place-based theories help to situate objects like the iPad as important contextually bound resources for play and meaning-making. Similarly, Rose, Fitzpatrick, Mersereau and Whitty (this volume) also emphasize and illustrate this material relationality between iPad minis, children, educators and the many *assemblages* enacted and provoked by the nature of inquiry pursuits of one early childhood classroom. In this volume, Winters and Memme discuss the ways in which iPads contribute to the discursive-construction of identity and positioning within children's socio-critical play and learning interactions. In addition, these two authors also provide practical insights associated with integrating iPads within an inviting, inquiry-based classroom context. Collectively, we all view the 21st-century child as capable and competent with a particular disposition towards technology (Harwood and Scott's discussion of digital habitus in this volume). We argue the digital habitus of children is unique given the technological culture they are a part of, challenging educators to recognize the ways in which children's ways of acting and being are shaped with/alongside technologies. Furthermore, the practical issues associated with integrating iPads within ECE are also highlighted; topics such as digital divides (Lane, this volume), diversity of learners (Di Cesare, Kaczorowski & Hashey, this volume), empowering readers and writers (Woloshyn, Grierson & Lane, this volume) and challenges associated with discerning quality within iPad applications (Di Cesare, this volume) are also considered.

Intentionally, the beginning chapters focus on the theoretical foundations supporting the research studies discussed and the researchers' framing. In the latter sections, the book offers practical insights and research-inspired stories of how young children think, play, experience and intra-act with digital worlds and technologies. iPads (among many other objects and other forms of technologies and mobile platforms) are important to young children. Hillevi Lenz Taguchi (2010) reminds us that the child and world are 'entangled becomings' (p. 47) – dynamic, mutually interdependent agents contributing equivalently to knowing. Consequently, as educators and researchers, we are challenged to find ways to appreciate the naturalized ways children move in and out, within, between and among these formal and informal spaces, both digital and non-digital.

2

BE THE 'I' IN iPad

iPads and the Children Who Love Them

Jennifer Rowsell

Abstract

This chapter tells the story of objects first, followed closely by the stories of children who love them. I have purposefully positioned the child to follow the object in both the title and opening sentence to make a point about epistemic shifts that have happened before our eyes and our impoverished policies and pedagogies that continue to constrain the potential of digital modes (Rowsell, Colquhoun & Maues, in press). The privileging of objects relates to the salient role of technologies and devices that occupy our time and attention. The focus on children derives from an intense period of research that I have been involved, specifically looking at how iPads afford young learners opportunities to think in quite different ways.

Keywords

Materialism/Post-humanism, Multimodality, Place-Based Theory/Resources

NEW EPISTEMOLOGIES FOR MEANING-MAKING

Drawing on data from the *Crayons and iPads* research project alongside other research studies, within this chapter I consider how thinking through iPads is different from thinking with a book. In doing so, the chapter begins with theories that push for new definitions of literacy and epistemologies for meaning-making. A series of authentic examples in classrooms where iPad thinking takes place is used to help illuminate these theories, and I conclude with some provocations and cautionary notes.

If a foray into the history of technologies from the book to wearable devices teaches us anything, it is the relationship between people and their objects that provides important insights about how we think and learn. People read, communicate, compose and play on/with/through technologies. During the *Crayons and iPads* research, it became clear that children learn through tablets and, as a research team, we seldom separated out the child from the iPad – the iPad and child worked relationally. Also, as objects, iPads do not privilege one mode over another; visuals facilitate thinking as much as hypertext facilitates thinking. Multimodality pushes for a balanced approach to meaning-making that acknowledges the multiple affordances and constraints of modes. Conceptually, Prinsloo (2005) also considered the place-based nature of technologies and tendency in new literacies research to underemphasize context. As a result, the chapter mobilizes three theoretical approaches – materialism/post-humanism, multimodality and place-based theories – to analyze how 'we think with the objects we love; we love the objects we think with' (Turkle, 2007, p. 3).

Materialism and Post-Humanism

There have been an increasing number of studies applying materialist perspectives in literacy studies (e.g., Buchholz, Shively, Peppler & Wohlwend, 2014; Honeyford, 2013; Kuby, 2013; Thiel, 2015). The allure of materialist and post-human approaches lies in the ways that they account for objects/texts as producing knowledge for and with a reader or audience. Materialist and post-humanist scholars (Barad, 2007; Hultman & Lenz Taguchi, 2010) interpret how enmeshed people are with objects and texts that surround them. Rather than viewing material objects (Gee, 1996) as passive or inert, scholars applying materialism to research argue that objects are performative agents (Gutshall & Kuby, 2013; Lenz Taguchi, 2010). Humans are certainly agential with objects that they render meaningful. Subjects and objects work in synchronicity, and, I would argue, a more grounded approach to learning explores how individuals work in a web of human–object activity.

Watching children engage in play, they move from one object to the next and the objects they play with are as implicated in the play as much as the child. This sea of activity can be complex and requires much more teasing out than what currently exists in studies. In literacy research, such theorizing about objects is referred to as the materialist turn (Barad, 2007). Thinking about materialist perspectives on literacy builds on the work of Deleuze and

Guattari and has been called rhizomatic approaches to literacy (Gutshall & Kuby, 2013; Leander & Boldt, 2013). Deleuze and Guattari (1987) described rhizomes as erratic subterranean root systems that produce shoots in unexpected ways and directions. Rhizomatic theory aligns with materialism with the concern for exploring how embedded and enmeshed meanings become realized when they are theorized in relation to humans with objects. Privileging the term 'rhizomatic' as opposed to linear or hybrid models emphasizes that there is an unpredictability and multidirectional nature to meaning-making that happens when a child, for instance, moves around a play area to make sense of his or her environment.

There are theorists in the area of ECE who have been doing this kind of research for some time. For example, Hultman and Lenz Taguchi (2010) analyze unclear borders between objects and children in the midst of sense-making, what they describe as relational materialism. Interrelationships frequently happen between objects and people, and these forces play a key role in how the body and mind work together to make meaning. As Hultman and Lenz Taguchi describe, 'an assemblage of forces and flows that emerge in interaction' (2010, p. 38). A materialist framework challenges assumptions that individuals drive meaning-making in isolation from material objects and defies perceptions of research as merely 'humanocentric' (Hultman & Lenz Taguchi, 2010, p. 39). Moving beyond a purely human perspective of research means locating learning more in contexts (rather than in people's heads and minds) and theorizing how individuals exist in social worlds.

Multimodality

Children's texts often have drawings, words, and young learners often talk as they draw. A theory of multimodality accounts for an equal emphasis on different modes of representation and expression to make meaning. Multimodality allows for ideas to be represented visually as well as in writing. The concept of multimodality grew out of semiotics – the study of signs – and the importance of seeing all sign making, or semiosis, as composed of an ensemble of modes. An idea can be drawn, enacted, modeled or spoken. A mode is one particular form in which it is possible to represent an idea. Sometimes it is easier to put an idea into a drawing rather than a piece of writing.

On an iPad, for example, visuals and animated text tend to be more pervasive than words. This idea of possibility in meaning-making can be described as an affordance. An affordance describes the specific possibilities that modes offer. With film, for example, there are more possibilities because there is sound, language, image, lighting and so on. This does not mean that one mode can do more than another. Rather, as Lemke (2000, 2002) describes, there is a multiplying effect of modes; modes build meanings. Scholars have taken up the challenge of multimodal literacies and have illustrated in their research how meaning-makers learn quite naturally through a variety of modes, sometimes in isolation and sometimes combined (Flewitt, 2008, 2011; Jewitt & Kress, 2003; Kress, 1997; Lancaster, 2003; Stein, 2008). Multimodal texts help to reveal the interests, motivations and an individual's pathway into literacy (Kress, 1997). Multimodal texts are infused with meanings and carry traces of their histories within them. Meaning-makers engage with text-making, and when they do so, they bring identities with them. In this way, multimodality can provide a wider understanding of text-making. For iPad research, taking a multimodal perspective to the research widens the analytical gaze to account for how children use and understand texts, apps, social media and other components of the iPad experience.

iPads AS PLACED RESOURCES

Thinking back to post-humanism, within a materialist paradigm, iPads are dynamic objects that are mediated in endlessly different ways by people in a multitude of contexts. Prinsloo (2005) identified a gap in new literacies research on how technologies exist in social contexts and the role of context in how technologies are used and understood. In a special issue on the topic, we (Prinsloo & Rowsell, 2012) illustrated how obfuscated place can be when conducting digitally based and technology-reliant research. In this special issue, researchers around the globe examined the role of place in how technologies are used across contexts (e.g., at home or in the community) within a specific location (e.g., rural Australia).

Given the connected, mobile nature of many technologies, they can be regarded as placeless, context-free when in fact, like all objects, technologies are informed by contexts as much as contexts are informed by technologies. Prinsloo (2005) advocates for a view of technologies as placed resources and avoiding universalizing the contexts where they are used. Prinsloo speaks specifically of new literacies scholars who tend 'to treat as given the processes of signification and meaning-making involved, which on closer examination turn out to be considerably more complex and variable than they suggest' (p. 3). His analyses of the placed nature of technologies worked on two levels. On one level, he notes how there is a general 'ignoring or at the very least backgrounding' of contextual factors in accounts of new literacies. Given the great potential for connectivity (Castells, 2000) with mobile devices, the skills derived from technology use are 'skills [that] are treated as something externally given, for the learner to "acquire"' (Prinsloo, 2005, p. 2). This is certainly not the case for developing countries where there are obstacles in terms of Wi-Fi and connectivity and access to technologies. From an African context, Prinsloo notes how technology use varies greatly and there is not a taken-for-granted status to Wi-Fi and to the kinds of technologies available to children and young people, clearly demonstrating how integral an account of context and situations can be when working within a 'new literacies' paradigm.

For studies presented in this chapter, the contexts involved a region of southern Ontario and an area outside of Toronto, Canada. For *Reading by Design*, the research study was situated closer to Toronto, with students mostly from white European middle-class backgrounds and minimal diversity. This research team examined the use of iPads in grade-3 and -6 classrooms (Rowsell & Gallagher, in press). For the two other research studies (*Crayons and iPads* and *Thinking Haptically: Tutoring with iPads*), these were situated in a small city in southern Ontario. To contextualize this research site, there are four smaller cities in close proximity with a rather homogenous population of white European Canadians from predominantly working-class backgrounds. Resources like iPads and high-end technologies cannot be taken for granted in this community, and many children do not have Wi-Fi access at home. These specificities provide insight into place and levels of access to technologies within communities. Keeping context in mind, I will now offer some telling instances of multimodal materialism in placed situations drawing from the three aforementioned research studies.

Virtual Grandma

A favourite excerpt from the *Crayons and iPads* study happened when researchers observed four children playing with the *Grandma's Kitchen* app. The app entails baking with a virtual grandma who dances and sends kisses as you bake, accompanied by other activities like making compound words or watching cooking video clips. Alongside playing *Grandma's Kitchen*, children went back and forth the pretend kitchen in the classroom to imitate what they did on-screen (Di Cesare, Harwood & Rowsell, 2016).

As with Rose, Fitzpatrick, Mersereau and Whitty's chapter in this collection, children observed in the kindergarten class also demonstrated naturalized movements between physical environments and virtual ones and back again. In Chapter 3, Rose et al. explore how children fluidly moved from outdoor spaces to iPad texts. Similarly, with *Grandma's Kitchen* the children also moved from virtual, multimodal texts (e.g., a video of people cooking) to physical objects (e.g., food toys) to emulate the practices they were watching

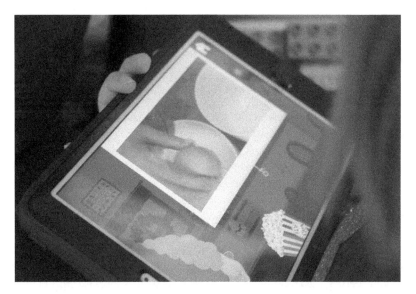

Figure 2.1 Grandma's Kitchen app

(Di Cesare et al., 2016). These actions and decisions were unprompted; they simply emerged from curiosity about what it might feel like to hold an (albeit pretend) egg, bowl and spoon. These fairly standard early-years practices (e.g., children playing in a pretend kitchen) were combined with playing an app and actually kissing the screen when virtual grandma offers a kiss, then transitioning to viewing a video and studying intently how to properly crack open an egg. These actions and thinking processes emulate my earlier discussion about a post-human turn in literacy studies. Burnett (2015) describes these multimodal mobilities as immaterializing literacy practices, or as she expresses it: 'I use the term *(im)materialities* to capture the way that the material and immaterial are always enmeshed with each other' (p. 520). Although the children cannot actually kiss grandma or stir real eggs, they have background knowledge, felt experiences or imaginings from their own experiences, books or movies to be able to show affect and to make meaning from them.

My argument here is that it is the material–immaterial interplay that ignites and animates thinking. The strength of visual, kineikonic/moving image, words and animations as modes with the haptic nature of their learning through tapping, scrolling, touching and so on culminates and combines to make this event happen. This 21st-century material–immaterial interplay results in quite a different rendition of meaning-making possibilities in comparison to children's previous experiences with playing in a pretend kitchen or cracking a real egg in a bowl. The point here is not that one is not better or preferable over another but rather that it is different and we have yet to fully understand what that difference is or what it means.

Billy, Olaf and Frozen

In the *Thinking Haptically* research study, tutors were a part of a tutoring program whereby teacher education students tutored children (adolescents and teenagers) in the community after school four nights a week. In our tutoring centre, we devoted one night a week to iPad tutoring and developing literacy skills through apps, short movies and podcasts, web-based texts, videogames and multimodal composing. During the winter session of 2015, Billy (all names are pseudonyms), a school-aged girl, worked with Sandra, a teacher education student, on iPad activities. Billy struggled with reading and writing and often found it hard to concentrate when she read longer texts. To respond to Billy's attention issues, Sandra chose to bolster her confidence by reading shorter texts with her and interspersing reading events with media texts such as short excerpts of films that she liked. After each tutoring session on iPad nights, tutors wrote reflections on our research blog. In one of the blog posts, Sandra talked about Billy's animated and lively reading of a book about Olaf from the popular Disney film, *Frozen*. Before reading the iBook, Billy talked about the movie and how much she loved Olaf the snowman because he was so funny in the movie. Then, she read the text, showed parts of the movie with Olaf, and sang *Let It Go* by Demi Lovato. The following is an excerpt from Sandra's reflective blog post of March 2015:

The next activity we did was reading on the iPad. We used the Disney Channel app, as Billy wanted to read the Olaf/Frozen books. We read the Olaf's Summer Day, which seemed to be a little too challenging for her, so we put the reading assist on. She really enjoys being read to. We then started to read Frozen, *Big Snowman Little Snowman*. She tried to tell me that it was too hard to read, but she was able to read this story well. She only really struggled with two words in the story. Using the same decomposition method, she made the words *thawed* and *apart*. Then, Billy wanted to watch Olaf on a YouTube video, and then we watched Elsa sing Let it Go! and Billy sang along. From my own observations of her reading, she performed better on the iPad, but she used pictures in the hard text to help her decode words.

Having observed this particular session and other sessions between Billy and Sandra, I became aware of how much Billy resisted reading because of her own struggles with reading at school. Her associations with reading tended to be about levelled texts, and she exhibited more engagement when Sandra diversified the reading process and combined reading with other multimodal texts. As with the last example from *Crayons and iPads*, Billy worked across modes and there was not a predictable, linear pathway to her reading, but instead it was much more hybrid in nature. On-task behaviours were maximized when Billy had some freedom and license to choose what she read – then view – then talk and interact. As an object, the iPad allowed her to engage in this kind of fluidity in her literacy work.

Jeremy and Minecraft

As a final example, I feature an excerpt from the *Reading by Design* study. The research participant featured is Jeremy, a school-aged boy, reading to me different genres and formats of texts on an iPad. The purpose of the one-on-one reading event in the research was to observe how Jeremy read across different genres of texts on a tablet. To begin with, Jeremy read a Canadian government website and he read it in a monotone voice and moved quickly to different parts of the text. What I observed as Jeremy read the print-heavy text is similar to what I have seen other readers do while reading on tablets – he treated the iPad like a book and put his finger beneath words and read along as an emergent reader might read a book. Later, I observed Jeremy read a shark interactive book and he showed some interest in the text, but it did not capture as much of his attention because there were not many interactive features, and when he tapped on text parts, they often did not respond. What I noted about this text is that he expected coloured text to be hyperlinked, so he would pause, look confused and move on when the text was not linked to new material. Reflecting on the event, Jeremy brought his prior knowledge about the interactive, multimodal nature of haptic texts on iPads to this reading event, but the text worked on book logic and not on screen logic and, as a result, he did not enjoy the experience.

However, the animated boy I had observed playing Minecraft displayed entirely different emotional and sensory reactions. As Jeremy played Minecraft, he was as focused as he was chatty and excited. While playing Minecraft, Jeremy created a story about a design that he planned to make around a particular lifestyle that he desired and he adapted his conception of this lifestyle into a specific design. When he moved into survival mode, he made his house into a fortress to protect it against a zombie invasion. Sitting next to readers like Jeremy for one-on-one readings of a variety of texts on an iPad consolidated a deeper understanding about the amount of design work that happens and not simply design work for aesthetic effects, but actual design work connected with storylines. Of the 15 different readers that I observed in-depth over a three-month period for the *Reading by Design* research, half of them were highly engaged in designing texts in Minecraft, Puppetpals or Toontastic. And with these designs, there were always story narratives that accompanied the designs. Clearly, there was print reading and language development, but it was the multimodal design work that took place that exhibited the most engagement by the children. Purely as an object, a book versus a tablet invites different types of expectations. Having observed Jeremy with an actual book and having observed him with a tablet, there are palpable differences on sensorial and intellectual levels.

BEING THE 'I' IN iPad … TOWARDS A NOTION OF *DIGITAL HABITUS*

So much of what we learn today in informal contexts is curated through auto-didactic measures and practices on technologies. Plainly speaking, we use our devices to seek out information on-demand (Rowsell, Colquhoun & Maues, in press) whenever we want it, and for many people, this is second nature. When we want to know anything, we are more likely to Google it on a smartphone or tablet to locate the information quickly than using a book or reference material or a library archive. A key insight from the many studies in the area of digital literacies is the DIY culture (Ito, Okabe & Matsuda, 2006; Jenkins, 2006) that technologies, search engines and social media have generated. In this volume, Harwood and Scott pursue the concept of a *digital habitus*. I too feel that this kind of framing of younger generations could be helpful. Small actions, knowledge production practices and even belief systems that people recruit through their use of digital technologies forge habits of mind-and-thought patterns which have shifted our dispositions to make meaning. I have argued in this chapter that learning to read and to process texts on tablets has changed the way we think. I deliberately elide more cognitive or neurological explanations to focus specifically on sociocultural changes in our patterns of thinking because I come from an ethnographic multimodal orientation to learning and teaching (Pahl & Rowsell, 2006). But, there are theorists like Carr (2010) who research how brains are changing based on contemporary reading patterns. Taking up Bourdieu's notion of habitus as 'an internalization of externality' (1980, p. 55) or as driving people's thoughts, perceptions, expressions and actions, can this notion be applied to digital practices? As a product of history, it is difficult to apply habitus to digital citizenship, but with technology (writ large) increasing its omniscience in our lives with each day, the ways in which devices like tablets shape knowledge and thoughts can soon be seen as our history.

Bourdieu (1980) argued that habitus embodies 'history, internalized as a second nature and so forgotten as history – [habitus] is the active presence of the whole past of which it is the product' (p. 56). Reflecting on this phrasing – internalized (thoughts, dispositions, even rituals) as second nature – calls to mind the second nature, naturalized practices of children involved in the *Crayons and iPads* project. Harwood has carved out a particular niche in theory and practice in the ways that she extrapolates how young children tacitly think and move across formal and informal spaces, engaging in complicated and sophisticated media practices – using the resources at hand to think and solve problems (Harwood, 2015). Over the course of tablet-based research, I have observed that learning is qualitatively different – it is lively, it is participatory, and it involves more than three modes at once. Might not these conditioned, spontaneous reactions and emotions be connected with histories and dispositions that unfold across contexts?

A central argument put forth in this chapter has been unravelling the specificities of tablet use and understandings both to demonstrate how idiosyncratic they are as objects and to push for a more ideological perspective on their foundational role in shaping practices (Rowsell & Wohlwend, 2016). There are certainly larger discussions about how humans and technologies have coevolved together (Hayles, 2012; Latour, 1992; McLuhan, 1964), but there is certainly more work to be done to understand how everyday objects like tablets and phones are enmeshed in networks of texts, practices, and improvisations of identity.

3

PLAYFUL PEDAGOGIC MOVES

Digital Devices in the Outdoors

Sherry Rose, Kristy Fitzpatrick, Candace Mersereau and Pam Whitty

Abstract

iPad minis were recently introduced to a group of 4-year-olds at the Children's Centre, University of New Brunswick (UNB), Fredericton. In this chapter, we explore how the children and their early childhood educators used these mobile devices outdoors in a nearby wooded area that the group adopted as an outdoor learning space. Concerns and complaints about increasing screen time for young children are often countered by a call to be 'in the outdoors'. Being in the outdoors then is constituted as a time away from the screen. We examine how the use of mobile devices in the outdoors can contribute to the deconstructing of this particular nature–culture binary (Taylor, 2013). Through critical revisiting of documentation and conversational records, we explore the following questions: How do educators and children employ digital tools, specifically the iPad mini in their daily outdoor learning encounters? What intra-actions occur in the woods inclusive of the children's interests, and how do they inform educators' pedagogic moves, or responsive strategies, in the context of iPad minis? What are the effects of these material intra-actions? What new questions arise?

Keywords

iPads and Outdoor Learning, Placed Resources, Assemblage Theory, Pedagogical Documentation, Nature–Culture Binary, Intra-actions and Pedagogies

INTRODUCTION

The Children's Centre in the Faculty of Education at the University of New Brunswick (UNB) was established in 1975. Conceived as a demonstration classroom for the early childhood program, the Centre welcomes 4-year-old children and their families, early childhood educators from universities and community college programs, and staff from schools and childcare centres across the province. As a demonstration site, the educators and professors working within the Centre are committed to innovative teaching, research and curriculum development. We have a longstanding history of critical reflection and complexifying early childhood pedagogies (Pacini-Ketchabaw, Nxumalao, Kocher, Elliot & Sanchez, 2015) through video and photo narrations of pedagogic encounters. Throughout any 1-year period, hundreds of conversations take place between the classroom educators and the early childhood professors at UNB. The learning in the classroom with the 4-year-olds is intricately connected to learning in the university classrooms, particularly early childhood literacies and curriculum. This chapter is both a collective and a collaborative, comprising our joint textualization within and through conversations, documentations and theoretical readings. The use of the word 'our' represents the productive and messy entanglements of multiple voices – two classroom educators, Kristy and Candace, and two teacher-educator professors, Sherry and Pam.

As part of the faculty contribution to the Centre's classroom and in the interest of exploring digital literacies, six iPad minis were purchased. The iPad minis are the perfect size for young children's hands and have sturdy covers that ensured durability for outdoor use. Our initial review of literature shaped our decision to use the iPad minis free of educational apps (Colbert, 2012) and as a placed resource (Prinsloo & Rowsell, 2012). In this chapter, we reflect upon 2 years of iPad mini usage through the revisiting of pedagogical documentations, conversations and conversational records. Taking up the theoretical positioning of the iPad mini as a placed resource helps us to 'consider the specificity of place and how mobile devices inflect local practices' (Rowsell et al., 2013, p. 351). Our initial specificities of place, in this instance, included the Early Childhood Children's Centre, our recently reconstituted playground and a nearby wooded area. We came to realize that when we placed the six iPad minis in the Centre, we naively had assumed that the iPad minis would replace cameras. We uncovered this assumption as we reviewed the documentation and noticed that iPad mini use was more frequent in the woods than on the playground. We attribute this in part to less tree coverage and more sun glare making iPad usage difficult on the playground. As well, there were challenges in accessing hotspots via the Internet, as it is dependent on the private communication plan on each individual's cellphone. Consequently, it is the nearby woods, which is the focus of the chapter.

THEORIES WE ARE THINKING WITH

As we reflect back on children and educators' iPad use, we find it difficult to maintain an isolated focus on the iPad as a specific technology. Theorizing the use of the iPad as a placed resource recognizes its mobility, as the device moves fluidly in and out of interaction with other mobile technologies, digital, human and more than human resources (Taylor, Pacini-Ketchabaw & Blaise, 2012). We found that our reflective rereadings and conversation around the documentation often slipped into what appeared to be an ecological approach, one where we caught ourselves privileging the iPad over the digital camera, books, oral language and other material relations.

In critically rereading and discussing the documented and oral learning encounters involving iPads, our attention turned to the material relationality between iPad minis, children, educators, bird skulls, animal tracks, bark stripping, clipboards, paper, pencils, moss, Shakespeare, witches, page protectors, letter patterns and much more found in the outdoors. We were examining assemblages that included the iPad mini. Our critical rereading of the documentation and our encounter with the work of Victoria Carrington (Marsh, 2014) brought us to theorize beyond an ecological approach and into the realm of assemblage theory. Carrington (2013) argues, 'While an ecological framing looks to find a contributory role for all components, an assemblage has room for tension, mismatch, and ongoing reconfiguration. There is not a sense of creating and maintaining a balanced symbiosis of parts. As a result of this heterogeneity and independence, assemblages dismantle and reassemble in different combinations as context and requirements shift' (p. 209). Theorizing with assemblage displaces the privileging of the iPad and opens space for us to (re)consider the dynamics of devices and their intra-actions with other materials used by the educators and children.

Henry Jenkins (2009) writes, 'injecting digital technologies into the classroom necessarily affects our relationship with every other communications technology, changing how we feel about what can and should be done with pencils and paper, chalk and blackboard, books, films, and recordings' (p. 7). In his work on digital technologies, Jenkins, a media studies scholar, theorizes extensively on participatory cultures. He defines participatory culture as 'cultures with relatively low barriers to artistic expression and civic engagement, strong support for creating and sharing creations, and some type of informal mentorship whereby experienced participants pass along knowledge to novices' (p. xi). The essential participatory cultures include play, performance, simulation, appropriation, multitasking, distributed cognitions, collective intelligence judgement, transmedia navigation, networking and negotiation (p. xiv). Many of these characteristics of participatory cultures are evident as we reread the documentation.

Our decision to focus upon outdoor spaces combined with our reading of Affrica Taylor's (2013) book, *Reconfiguring Childhoods*, challenged us to examine the relationship between nature and culture. An example of the nature–culture binary occurred when we first introduced the iPads. Some parents viewed digital technologies as a threat to children's active participation, social engagement and their children's use of traditional early childhood learning materials. Working with Taylor's reconceptualization of naturecultures and Carrington's explication of assemblages, we ask how do iPads, children, educators and the living and inert non-human others mutually affect each other?

RESEARCH APPROACH

Methodologically, we reviewed, selected and critically interpreted pedagogical documentation from the 2 years of iPad mini usage at the centre. Pedagogical documentation was an unfolding rhizomatic narrative practice that the UNB Children's Centre had developed over the past decade. Pedagogical documentation – the narration of our educational encounters with children through video, photographs, artefacts and texts – is argued to be one way to listen, recollect, question, reimagine and re-enact our moral, ethical and relational responsibilities that contribute to and sustain children and adult's flourishing. Documentation of children's learning, as it is situated in the *New Brunswick's Curriculum for Early Learning and Child Care-English* (2008), has been profoundly influenced by the work of Reggio Emilia in northern Italy (Rinaldi, 2004), learning stories in the Te Whariki curriculum framework of Aotearoa–New Zealand (Carr, 2001; Carr and Lee, 2012), the Swedish preschool curriculum (Dahlberg & Lenz Taguchi, 1994; Olsson, 2009), and Project Zero and Reggio Children (Krechevsky, 2004).

Pedagogical documentation narratives make explicit subjective relational moments too often silenced by rationalities of individualism, standardization and universalisms (Rose, 2012). Necessary processes to realizing the transformative work of pedagogic documentation include open listening, critical dialogue and public theorizing that seeks out diverse perspectives, viewing uncertainties and seeing silences and dissensus as possibilities not dangers (Hughes & MacNaughton, 2000). Because the identities of the learners who produced the narrative are often at stake, as they are with most educational practices, documentation processes are grounded in relational ethics – an ethics of encounter (Levinas, 1989), a pedagogy of listening (Rinaldi, 2004), a respect for being, becoming and belonging, and a commitment to cultivate participatory spaces (Moss, 2014).

For us, this researching process included formal meetings, informal conversations and reviewing of pedagogical documentations – with the goal of understanding how children and educators were taking up the iPad mini as placed resource. Our collective conversations uncovered that iPad mini usage was influenced by accessibility to the Internet, the use of iPad more often in the woods than on the playground, and greater use in warmer weather. From pedagogical documentation, we selected specific narratives that involved the use of iPad minis, cellphones and digital cameras in our nearby wooded area. Putting pedagogical documentation to work, as a research approach, means engaging in joint theorizing, co-authoring and co-questioning of narrative documentations (Pacini-Ketchaw, 2015; Rinaldi, 2004; Rose, 2012). This joint theorizing can be fraught with productive tensions, exuberant possibilities, ethical questions and disquieting contradictions, while creating a communal space for valuing the participations of children, parents and educators necessary to realizing educational goals while negotiating ethical responsibilities together (Dahlberg, Moss & Pence, 2007; Edmiston, 2008).

RESEARCHING DOCUMENTATION

Our simultaneous reading of the literature on iPad minis in concert with our joint researching resulted in convergent themes for theorizing drawn from the literature. These themes include imaginative play; iPad as research tool; and playful experimentation with the devices. In the next section of the chapter, we discuss these themes individually, and then within the context of 'The Evil Witches', we demonstrate the intra-active workings of the three themes.

Imaginative Storytelling

There has been a longstanding practice for Centre educators to support children's storytelling through traditional props such as felt boards, daily poetry, frequent recital of storied and poetic refrains, and inviting children to tell and perform their own stories. When children and adults filmed children's storytelling on an iPad mini, there was instant playback where they could view their productions and share them with others. They watched each other's productions, those of their friends, and shared this documentation/production with parents and educators.

iPad Mini as Research Tool

As we reviewed the documentation, we noticed that over the past 2 years the iPad was a research tool supporting children's inquiries. Children and adult inquiries are integral to pedagogical practice in the Centre, and pedagogical narration deepens and traces inquiries. In the narration of *Tracks and Scat*, the

Figure 3.1 Pocket Guide to Identify Tracks

iPad mini was used to photograph tracks and scats before they were stepped on, and left unrecognizable.

Photos of the tracks and scat allowed the children to have an up-close look without touching. The photo was then used alongside track identification pocket guides, so the children could determine which animal left the track or scat (Figure 3.1). Working with the iPad mini provided the benefit of being able to zoom in on the track or scat to have a closer, more detailed look.

In the pedagogical narration of *Skull and Cocoon*, the iPad was used to research which animal the skull hailed from or which animal had made the cocoon. Again, laminated identification charts helped children identify trees, leaves, scat, tracks and skeletons. These charts were in frequent use by both children and adults to identify new discoveries made in the woods. In addition, key thoughts and ideas from the woods were recorded in an outdoors journal (Figure 3.2). The format of the journal was textual, visual and artefactual. The children compared images found on Google to the skull or cocoon found in the woods to determine the related animal or insect. The iPad mini served as an identification resource offering immediate and fluid research options, often with more examples and details, exceeding the educators and children's knowledge as well as the information contained on the paper identification charts.

Figure 3.2   Recording in an Outdoor Journal

Playful Experimentation

The iPad mini, in the hands of the children, also resulted in photographs of themselves in child-sized spaces such as the hollowed-out stump of a tree. In another instance, a child playfully narrated his own actions as he filmed, claiming his documentation was like a YouTube video (Figure 3.3). One girl created spontaneous songs and replayed them, and many of the children enjoyed the playfulness of taking their picture and manipulating the images in multiple ways constituting a form of dizzy play (Kalliala, 2006). To illuminate these themes further, we turn to a fuller examination of a documentation entitled *The Evil Witches*.

Figure 3.3   Playful Experimentation

The Evil Witches Narration

This narration is an example of imaginative storytelling, playful experimenta-tion and the use of iPad minis as a research tool; the three themes intra-acting to support the children's evil witches play. Daily, children play in a wooded area just in front of the Centre. On the initial day of the evil witch play, a couple of children transformed hollowed-out stumps into baking and cooking vessels. Becoming evil witches, they began baking lovely cakes and cooking poisonous soups, stirring while they cackled and claimed to kill the people who ate the soups they served.

As Candace, their educator, watched and listened, she joined the chil-dren's play world reciting the refrain from the witches scene in Act 1, Scene IV from Shakespeare's *Macbeth*. 'Double, double, toil and trouble. Fire burn and cauldron bubble.' As Candace wrote in her observation notes, 'I already had the iPad to take photos of them, so I quickly turned on the hotspot on my cellphone, connected the iPad mini to the internet and searched for the full witches' song in the play.' The next time the children came to the woods, Candace brought the full version of the witch song, Act IV Scene I from Shakespeare's *Macbeth*.

As Candace reread Shakespeare's original witches text, repeating the refrain, 'Double, double, toil and trouble. Fire burn and cauldron bubble', one of the children identified Candace as 'The witch who reads the recipe', deliberately drawing Candace deeper into their play world. Over time and repeated chant-ing, the children began to question the meaning of words and phrases from the 17th-century play. Using the iPad, Candace and the children looked up the following phrases; fenny snake, eye of newt, howlet's wing and adder's fork. The use of the iPad provided immediate and accessible visual responses to the children's questions, searching for pictures of creatures or vocabulary they were unfamiliar with, such as newts and adders.

With the addition of this very specific information, the children began remix-ing the poetic recipe, substituting Shakespeare's ingredients with items found in the immediate areas of woods in which they were playing. A new composi-tion unfolded as Candace and the children co-constructed a poetic recipe for Poison Soup. 'Moss for the bat fur' Julia, one of the children proclaimed. 'We are born evil witches!' another child, Ana, cackled! Candace quickly recorded the child-witches' ingredients.

Poison Soup
'Moss for bat fur
Ice for people

Mud for fire to burn

Sticks for snakes

Toes are pine needles

Eye of lizard is tiny pieces of wood

Put everything in the pot.

Stir it up.

We say: 'Double, Double, toil and trouble;

Fire burn and cauldron bubble:

Then we give it to people and they die.'

Once back in the classroom, Candace sealed the recipe in a page protector to keep it safe for outside use. She added a copy of the original poem and an illustration from *Poetry for Young People: William Shakespeare* in another protected sleeve. Both recipes, the child and Shakespearean compositions, were protected, and the children's and Shakespeare's composing are aligned and made portable to travel into the woods. Many times throughout the weeks of the witches play, the iPad mini acted in support of imaginative storytelling, research and playful exploration. The following is another example that occurred in the spring.

Evil Witches: Ice Expedition

Today, as we began to play in the witches' house with our cauldron,? Janice exclaimed, 'This is a winter recipe! We don't have any ice anymore'. 'Are you certain?' Candace questioned her. 'Do you think there may be a place deep in the dark wood where there may still be some snow and ice hiding?' 'Let's go check!' Janice answered, 'but how will we not get lost?' Candace explains, 'On my phone, I have something called a compass. When you are travelling, the Earth has 4 directions: North, South, East, and West. The compass has a needle that will point in the direction you are headed. We will mark our place here and then use the compass to always make sure we are headed back in this direction to this spot.' Once we had our bearings, we set off in the woods in search of ice and snow.' Janice wanted to take the iPad and document our journey to show Jill when we got back. Because she took so many pictures, she and I sat down to sort through them and decided which to keep and which to delete. (*Documentation-Candace*, May 2014)

CRITICAL REFLECTION

Jenkins (2009) draws upon James Gee's (2004) concept of *affinity spaces* as sites where powerful opportunities for learning are sustained through common endeavours that bridge differences in age, class, race, gender, educational level. The witch play is one such affinity space where child, adult, iPad, moss, Shakespeare, stumps, ice, pine cones and sticks sustained imaginative storytelling, research and playful experimentation as the children remixed Shakespeare text into their own witch recipe. In these spaces, individuals participate in various ways according to their skills and interests. Participation depends on peer-to-peer teaching with individuals motivated to acquire new knowledge or refine existing skills; affinity spaces allow each participant to feel like an expert while tapping each other as resources. How do affinity spaces work? What are the intra-actions of the materialities of the outdoor environments and digital environments? What are the effects of these intra-actions? What do these assemblages produce?

In *The Evil Witches* documentation, Candace responded to the children's witch play, which may be provoked by the wooded area. The tree stump calls up a cauldron and the woods themselves call up children's prior story experiences with dark, dark woods represented in the tales they read. Gee (2004) explains that affinity spaces are different from formal schooling spaces given the dynamic, innovative and experimental nature, whereby the informal learning community seeks to respond to localized short-term needs and temporary interests. The woods offer a learning space that is quite different from the classroom. The space as a generative environment implies that the materiality of trees, stumps, moss, leaves, sticks form an intra-action with the children and educator's experiences and imagination, evoking new aesthetic experiments and creativity. Candace calls forth her memory of Macbeth in response to the children's witch play. Both Candace and the children use the iPad to research the full chant of Macbeth's witches; they investigate the new vocabulary and look up visuals of unknown animals and document their own ice expedition.

The documentation details a fluidity of both time and texts. Across four centuries and over several days of the children's lives, they move across multiple texts – digital, oral, poetic – as they create their recipe. All these texts become mobile as they travel into and out of the woods. Together, the children and Candace generate a learning, playing, and creative space as they compose play worlds and texts together, drawing from a high school text. Exploring children's and educators' play with digital technologies, including iPads, cameras and cellphones, demands attention to the context in which the engagement occurs, the form of the activity, its place in young children's play repertoires and the conditions which promote sustained and meaningful encounters (Stephen & Plowman, 2014). When we considered the Children's Centre context in which these digital engagements occurred, there pre-exists a high degree of curiosity and playfulness evident in the examples provided.

The collaborative cultural productions detailed in *The Evil Witches* docu-mentations never privileged reading, writing, designing or playing; rather, each of these processes combined in assemblages of literacies in moment-to-moment interactions (Wohlwend & Medina, 2014). Children's and educators' co-creations as represented in the documentations are 'fragments of children's learning which spur thought, curiosity and understanding' (Pacini-Ketchabaw et al., 2015, p. 2). In this chapter, the documentation provided insights about what digital tools were selected and how the devices were used outdoors. Each of these encounters illustrated a move 'away from a world where some few produce and many consume media toward one in which everyone has a more active stake in the culture that is produced' (Jenkins, 2009, p. 12).

As Carrington (2013) theorizes, 'assemblages dismantle and re-assemble in different combinations as context and requirements shift' (p. 209). Contrary to some popular beliefs, Plowman & Stevenson (2012) and Vanderwater (2007) found that children's interactions with digital devices do not silence other forms of play. Children often balance (or converge) their interactions with digital devices with their ongoing play, in this case the witch play. Digital play-fulness can work with children's play pursuits, particularly when those digital interactions are sensitively guided, multimodal and combined with resources that are intentionally chosen by the educator in response to children's actions, questions and passions (Stephen & Plowman, 2014).

As a beginning step, we illustrate *The Evil Witches* documentation as a means of deconstructing the nature–culture binary that appears in the literature in rela-tion to nature and technology. Moreover, *The Evil Witches* illustrates a second deconstruction in the adult–child binary often present with children's playful imaginings. For example, a child-initiated pedagogic move occurred when the children named Candace as the recipe-reading witch. By so doing, they fluidly moved Candace beyond her pedagogic desire to deepen their play to becom-ing a player. This positioning as an adult-player is theorized by Brian Edmiston (2008) as essential to creating a social aesthetic space where children and adults co-author understanding and, over time, shape and form ethical identities.

THEORETICAL TROUBLING

Brian Edmiston (2008) writes:

> When children play, in imagination, they fully enter worlds that may be engag-ing and complex as the cultural narratives that they draw upon include their re-told experiences, the stories they have read, and the movies they have watched. When adults play with children they can likewise enter those worlds

not to observe but to participate with children, not only to listen but to interact and shape meaning, and not only to enter imagined space-times but to explore possible ways of acting and identifying with other people in the world. (p. 12)

In the context of *The Evil Witches*, the question of what 'cultural narratives' we choose to play remains to be troubled. In her work, Taylor (2013) introduces 'commonworlds' as a way to bring nature and culture back together disrupting this longstanding binary – a binary reiterated when digital technologies are positioned against outdoor play. Taylor questions, 'How might we approach the relationship of childhood and nature without rehearsing nostalgic adult idealizations, sentimental attachments or heroic rescue and salvations appeals?' (p. 63). Commonworlds theorizing also raises deeper questions that would trouble our account and are perhaps an investigation for another telling of the witch tale – a telling that would put a stutter into the focus of digital documentations. Questions such as: What are the First Nations histories of place that are silenced by our colonial histories of Shakespeare, early childhood pedagogies, and human-centric ontologies? What are the biographies of the creatures that live in dying stumps? What are the histories of this place that are silenced as we are caught in the remixing of a familiar imaginative play space?

4

DIGITAL INQUIRY AND SOCIO-CRITICAL NEGOTIATIONS IN TWO EARLY CHILDHOOD CLASSROOMS

Kari-Lynn Winters and Leslie Memme

Abstract

Inquiry has long been an essential component in early-years classrooms. Digital tablets add another dimension to this experience. While handling mobile tablets, some of these socio-critical interactions during play are positive and collaborative; others are more challenging and require children to take stances and discursive positions in order to negotiate ideas and emotions. Power is not always equally distributed. Specifically, this chapter looks at how young children from two early-years classrooms in southern Ontario negotiated social interactions with their peers when children had the opportunities to use iPads. Findings from this ten-month study suggest that even young children have the capacity to position each other and take on perspectives in order to navigate these digital and socio-critical participatory spaces with nuanced complexity.

Keywords

Discursive Positions, Social Interactions, Perspective Taking

SOCIAL POSITIONING IN THE KINDERGARTEN CLASS

It was a typical Thursday morning for Mrs. Walden's kindergarten class (all names that appear in the chapter are pseudonyms). Children were scattered about the large room, focusing on various activities and materials laid out as part of the Children's Centre time activities (e.g., musical instruments, writing tasks, tablets). Four boys were building airplane-like vehicles on two iPads, using a Lego Builder app. This was the fifth time these kindergarten-aged children had experienced the tablets as part of a classroom inquiry about transportation. Though these children were cooperating better than they had in the previous research visits, they were observed negotiating power and positioning of each other within their situated context.

Vignette #1: Make It Fly

Mark: Did you know that we could add feet?

Jerry: Add feet?

Mark: I wanna try.

Mark takes the tablet from Jerry and fiddles with the tablet. Jerry continues to touch the screen of the tablet as well. Andy watches and follows along on his own tablet.

Andy: Oh! And propellers.

Mark takes the tablet back from Jerry and looks for propellers. Luke leaves the table and returns with actual Lego pieces. He looks at the tablet and back to his Lego, pulling out the pieces he needs. Jerry watches.

Jerry: I want that one (grabbing a few Lego pieces).

Andy: I know how to get lots of stuff (fiddling with his tablet).

Luke: Yes, and … but there's not enough pieces. But …

Luke grabs the tablet from Andy and tries to build a replica of what he sees on the screen.

Everyday classroom activities among young children involve negotiations of power and social positioning (Dyson, 1997; Lensmire, 2000; Stein, 2008; Vratulis & Winters, 2013). The above vignette illustrates the types of interactions the authors observed during a ten-month study (entitled *Crayons and iPads*) in two ECE classrooms. This chapter not only demonstrates the ways that digital technologies (specifically iPads) affect classroom dynamics, but it also illustrates how learners make sense of everyday experiences and how these interactions socially position children in particular ways.

Results outlined in this chapter are specific to the two classrooms where the authors observed and interviewed the children, documented with photos and videos and conversed with the teachers. Here in Mrs. Walden's classroom, the boys were cooperating, laughing and calling out to show one another what they were doing. They moved fluidly between the actual building of the Lego and the virtual building on their app, positioning themselves and each other as digital explorers and knowers of information within their situated context. At times, they claimed ownership and snatched the iPads from one another. Over time they did negotiate and find a way to make their vehicles fly. Collaboratively, they talked about the app features, used their imaginations to replicate and fly their real-life constructions and eventually added their constructions to the vehicle museum for the classroom.

Socio-critical experiences have long been explored within literacy classrooms, including the ways that children participate together, negotiate social activities, assume perspectives and position others (e.g., Dyson, 1997; Lensmire, 2000; Wells, 1999). However, as recent research demonstrates (e.g., Falloon & Khoo, 2014; Lynch & Redpath, 2014; Vasquez & Felderman, 2013), digital technology, iPads in particular, add another dimension to this experience. For example, Fisher, Lucas and Galstyan (2013) argue that the unique features of iPads with their touchscreen interfaces, portable designs, wireless connectivity, multiple viewing angles and wide array of apps not only promote learner collaborations but also allow users to transition fluidly between public and private work spaces, therefore sharing information and embodied engagement. In addition, Falloon (2013a) shows the transformed ways children engage in decision-making when devices are included in specific learning situations. Though at times the students got distracted by the apps, and occasionally frustrated (e.g., limited reading abilities, lack of technical support), Falloon makes a compelling argument that iPads are indeed powerful learning tools that enhance motivation and learner engagement. Specifically, when using the iPads, the 5-year-old children in Falloon's study consistently wove rich interactions between their background experiences, prior knowledge and the content of the apps themselves, as well as they explored diverse cognitive, social and emotional problem-solving pathways within their social contexts.

INQUIRY-BASED PEDAGOGIES AND SOCIO-CRITICAL NEGOTIATIONS

Classrooms that promote inquiry, whether virtual or actual, often encourage active explorations, authentic questioning and real-life problem-solving (Bruce & Casey, 2012; Chiarotto, 2011). These classrooms incorporate children's playful insights and interests, the educators' intentions and learning goals, as well as objectives of larger pedagogical frameworks set in place by schools and school boards (Harwood, Bajovic, Woloshyn, Di Cesare, Lane & Scott, 2015). In addition, we suggest an inquiry-based pedagogy is one that focuses on 'possibility thinking' (Craft, 2000). The approach integrates an imaginative framework where learning is investigated, questioned, embodied and played out in order for learners to figure out or make sense of the world around them. Within an inquiry pursuit, learners work together, pose and solve problems, as well as discover and make connections with lived experiences. In its application, inquiry occurs in a shared space where children can encounter 'what if' experiences and explore self-actualization as well, bringing into existence the situated context, as well as the children's own identities and imagination. In this way, an inquiry-based pedagogy innately encourages originality, collective collaboration and socio-critical negotiation within situated contexts.

Social hierarchies during an inquiry process are not uncommon. This is because within collaborative spaces, children take on perspectives and 'indicate a stance toward experiences and ideas' in order to question and find collective answers that make sense to them (Wells, 1999, p. 121). Children move fluidly between the acts of cooperating, disputing, bargaining, managing, following, sharing and so forth, where power is not always equally distributed.

Cromdal (2001) observed that while exploring a topic, school-aged children establish participatory rights, as well as rules for cooperative play; they often claim ownership over materials and spaces, while socially accepting and rejecting each other's ideas during the process. Claiming ownership over materials and social activities enables children to determine how an inquiry will be explored, who is in charge of it and what rules might be considered important. Cobb-Moore, Danby and Farrell (2009) add that even young children consistently develop and use rules to control or understand the negotiations of their peers when working with materials and resources. Thus, children are never passive recipients within inquiries; rather, they use a variety of strategies to actively and competently enact regulation.

Socio-critical negotiations of power occur in classrooms regardless of whether technology is used. However, portable devices (e.g., tablets, cameras, smartphones) bring forth unique decision-making communications and circumstances (Luce-Kapler, 2006). The combination of tablet design features, the potential to be connected to local and global worlds simultaneously, and diverse options for content generation offered by various apps allow children to participate as valuable co-creators. Wohlwend (2013), for example, shows how children can simultaneously produce and disseminate digital productions, positioned as media makers (co-authors) rather than passive recipients. While touching screens, swiping and manipulating keyboards together, children discuss, play and design collaboratively. At times they also debate and refute each other too, as the voice of authority is not always equally available to all learners.

Vratulis and Winters (2013) found that portable digital devices became the catalyst for authentic, student-driven co-authorship, as the children in their studies were able to self-select and design their own opportunities for learning and to negotiate different entry points for content knowledge. They noted that although students would sometimes physically overtake the material resources (e.g., press virtual buttons, become possessive over digital equipment) and argue about or defend their choices, these socio-critical and digital interactions 'became powerful vehicles for students to advocate their positions and rationalize their thinking processes' (p. 102). Similarly, Falloon and Khoo (2014) posit that iPads stimulate unique collaborations and build increased exploratory talk. They suggest that interactions of iPad design features and open-design apps can provide a useful medium for helping learners master skills and support exploratory talk, ultimately constituting motivational and engaging skill practice environments. Inquiries and social negotiations are always relational, based on contexts and actions and the stories the children narrate within these spaces.

SUBJECT POSITIONS AND STORYLINES

When socially negotiating, children take on stances and layer 'subject positions' – affiliations (e.g., I am a woman, but also a mother, a writer, a professional and so forth). Subject positions incorporate both a conceptual repertoire and a location for people to use that repertoire (Davies & Harré, 1990, p. 46). In other words, these imagined and discursive roles are formed by: (1) the individuals who assume and assign stances and affiliations; (2) the immediate social circumstances; and (3) the larger cultural resources and repertoires of experiences that are brought to the situated context. In this way, when observing subject positions during research, it is important to look at the study participant, his/her locally constituted circumstances and any broader cultural influences (e.g., classroom climate, socioeconomic context); this is because as Anderson (2009) suggests (referencing Barth), 'classroom interactions and the various facets of a student's battery of positions are oriented over time and across multiple, interrelated contexts' (p. 293).

Within subject positions, perspectives are formed as people narrate their own point of view, assert and relinquish power and ultimately create storylines in order to make sense of social hierarchies and to understand their worlds. Davies and Harré (1990) suggest these critical and sophisticated acts of communication involve social intention and actions, whereby the identities of the participants are (to some extent) discursively constructed. Once having taken up a particular position as one's own, a person inevitably sees the world from the vantage point of that position and in terms of particular images, metaphors, storylines and concepts which are made relevant within the particular discursive practice in which they are positioned. Kultti and Odenbring (2015) extend this idea to children; they suggest that young children also have the capacity to construct in-the-moment social relations and discursively position themselves within social hierarchies.

Holland, Lachicotte, Skinner and Cain (1998) combine ideas of subject positions, storylines, agency and identity in their research. Specifically, they examine how identities are culturally constructed through the narratives individuals script, arguing that self-actualization (identity-making) is never static or linear, but interactive, variable and sometimes chaotic. Likewise, Winters (2012) proposes that the storylines that children narrate to themselves and to others shape aspects of both their fixed (e.g., gender, age) and flexible identities (e.g., popularity, group belonging). Her study demonstrated how a young boy's identity was shaped by the stories he constructed and the subject positions he assumed and assigned in his daily life. Winters' research illustrates that while children narrate storylines and interact socially, they also formulate and formalize their identities, and at the same time participate in larger cultural dialogues. Thus, the same child can simultaneously enact a variety of positions – 'multiplicity of selves' (Davies & Harré, 1990, p. 48) – while at the same time constructing a nuanced identity.

Since 1990, researchers have used Davies and Harré's and Holland's positioning and identity theories to explain classroom interactions and to show that identities are shaped through agency and lived practice (Anderson, 2009; Davies & Hunt, 1994; Winters, McLauchlan & Fournier, 2015). Winters and Vratulis (2012) draw upon these theories, for example, to explore how the storylines their study participants narrated gave them impetus to constitute and reconstitute diverse subject positions and to influence the perspectives these children took on, and sometimes challenged.

THE STUDY CONTEXT

In the *Crayons and iPads* study, the children we spent our time observing were mainly Caucasian, from lower to middle-class Catholic families, enrolled in one of two kindergarten classrooms. This was the first year of formal schooling for many of these children (ages 3–5). The classroom followed an inquiry-based curriculum model that provided time and resources for children to engage in freely chosen pursuits based on emerging questions such as: What lives in the ocean? How do movie theatres work? And where do babies come from? The children used a range of materials to explore these topics, including the digital iPads the research team provided. For example, in Mrs. Grange's class, the children used overhead projectors and markers, as well as Q-tips, construction paper and glue to explore two-dimensional skeletons. Later, the children had opportunities to extend their research on the skeletal system using the iPads. These children also had numerous opportunities to choose from a variety of play centres, such as wooden blocks, dramatic play or visual arts activities, or exploring with iPads. More structured activities, such as letter writing, counting and addition activities, and science explorations were encouraged by the educators as well and often included higher teacher involvement. Both classrooms were active and sometimes noisy as there were many inquiries occurring simultaneously and because the children could move about the room as they pleased. We found that the children were often collaborative and highly engaged in their own projects. For these reasons, this atmosphere provided rich opportunities for researching digital, participatory and socio-critical spaces.

The intent of the *Crayons and iPads* study was to capture children's everyday experiences and inquiries, including the children's use of materials, relationships and social orders within the situated contexts. The focus of the study was not on the devices themselves but rather more on the ways that young children interacted, worked together, refuted one another's ideas, or problem-solved when working with digital tablets – the negotiations behind the screen. For this reason, the researchers took a qualitative participant-observer approach to data collection, at times taking part in the activity (e.g., demonstrating how to use an app while photographing or taking notes) and sometimes assuming a bystander role.

BRINGING iPads INTO CLASSROOMS: OPPORTUNITIES AND CHALLENGES

Throughout our research visits, we did note that the tablets shaped unique social negotiations, providing both opportunities and challenges for the children. These findings aligned with other research studies that explored the potentials of iPads within schooled settings (Falloon & Khoo, 2014; Getting & Swainey, 2012; Miller, Krockover & Doughty, 2013). For instance, in Mrs. Walden's classroom we observed that the children seemed more motivated and enthusiastic about printing the alphabet in ways that were not observed before the tablets were introduced. Perhaps this new motivation was founded because the technology was exciting and the learning was more tailored to students' needs. For example, if a child could not hold a pencil, they could first print on the iPad with their finger, then practice with a stylus before moving to pencil and paper. The children also seemed to enjoy how easy it was for them to erase and rewrite the letters, as opposed to the more daunting finality of pencil to paper (even though erasers were available). In addition, the tablets allowed for immediate access to information through multiple modalities; in this way children with special needs were included in social negotiations, and the iPads provided new opportunities for collaboration.

Challenges with the iPads were also observed during our study. Other researchers too have experienced such difficulties when tablets were introduced into school settings. For example, Falloon and Khoo (2014) noticed that during social interactions some children were more focused on getting their responses right rather than building an authentic answer. Falloon (2014), in a separate study, noted students' difficulties with distractive app features (e.g., colourful popups, responsive animations) and struggles, persevering when apps became more challenging. In our study, we encountered challenges with the sharing of the devices. The vignette below demonstrates one of the struggles that were commonplace.

Vignette #2: I want it

Mary: (reaching for an iPad) I want it.

Ryan: Me too.

Educator: You can use it together.

Mary: But how do I get it to …

Gord: (pushing child #1's hands off the screen) I know how.

Ryan: I know how too. We have one at my house. My dad lets …

Gord: Push that one. I like that game.

Mary: Hey! No fair.

When the iPads were first introduced to the children, they had their own intentions and everyone wanted a turn at the same time. Some hunched over the tablets, almost in a protective mode. It was not uncommon to see children push other children's hands away from the screens (Figure 4.1). Here, the children negotiated with one another in physical ways that were relatively unproductive. The novelty and scarcity of the resources (few iPads), limited time, lack of explicit guidelines in regard to social navigations, as well as the classroom culture and layout were all contributing factors to the unsuccessful initial attempts to introduce iPads into these kindergarten classrooms. Falloon and Khoo (2014) also stress the importance of an early establishment of guidelines in regard to how students are expected to work together.

The above vignette also illustrates how some children positioned themselves as mentors (e.g., 'I know how …'), creating storylines about how they needed to take on a leader-like stance since they were older or more experienced with using tablets. Figure 4.1 depicts how children physically removed another's hands from the device. Others positioned themselves as amateurs (e.g., 'But how do I …?'). Indeed, for some children, this was the first time they had gained an opportunity to operate an iPad. Lack of experience with the iPads frustrated some, especially those that were used to taking charge

Figure 4.1   Pushing hands off screens

(e.g., 'Push that one ...'). The educators also found students with lack of experience frustrating, particularly with some of the more technical aspects of the iPads (e.g., how to take a screenshot).

PARTICIPATORY SPACES: MENTORSHIP AND COLLABORATIVE INQUIRY

Over time, as the learners became more comfortable with the iPads and also with a school purchase of more devices, we noticed increased mentorship and collaborative inquiry among the children (e.g., Vignette #1). After the initial weeks of the study, the iPads provided participatory spaces where sharing, exploring and the expression of learning happened. Also referred to as an 'affinity space' (Gee, 2004), the classroom can become a participatory and invitational space where 'learners apprentice themselves with a group of people who share certain practices (e.g., learning to cook in a family) ... and pick up these practices through joint action with more advanced peers, and advance their abilities to engage and work with others in carrying out such practices' (p. 70).

iPads can open up spaces for all children to assume subject positions as experts. The research vignette below illustrates how multiple children informed each other and participated in the space together, negotiating their own world experiences as they played. The children who had overheard the dialogue were drawn in and willingly participated. According to Gee (2004), people come together in participatory spaces not because of their race, gender or age but because they have an affinity to the content of a discussion or social action.

Vignette #3: Grandma, Nana, and Nona

Once during the study, we noticed two children standing beside one another in the dramatic play centre, exploring Grandma's kitchen app on their own tablets.

Anna: 'I'm playing the Nana game.'

Ryan: 'The Grandma Game?'

            This sparked a side bar conversation between two other learners who had not been actively participating in the original play session.

Mick: (turning around): 'I call my Grandma, Nana.'

Mary: (calling out): 'I don't have a Grandma; I have a Nona.'

EQUAL POWER: CREATING MIRRORED IDENTITIES WITH iPads

Sometimes physical and virtual spaces can mirror one another – also called converged spaces (Edwards, 2013b). Harwood et al. (2015) describe these as spaces where learning is 'accomplished with a "real" and "concrete" experience prior to, alongside or following a digitally mediated experience, often blurring different types of play and ultimately promoting the construction of unique understandings' (p. 60).

The children in one class created a movie theatre, including posters for new movies, a schedule and a ticket booth. Children participated freely in this centre, assuming roles as ticket sellers and movie actors. This inquiry merged with a virtual space when a story app (i.e., Puppet Pals) was introduced. Here, children chose the backgrounds and characters for their production. They recorded their voices to represent the characters in the narratives. They collaborated in similar patterns to the play observed in the dramatic play centre. Children participated in scenes together, elaborating on each other's story and the app's narrative at the same time. Power positions were distributed equally – so much so that the children finished each other's sentences. They positioned each other as capable and evil wizards. Imagination was fore-fronted during this inquiry. The children collaborated inside and outside of the production and demonstrated effective oral communication and presentation skills. These collaborations align with other studies (Falloon & Khoo, 2014; Harwood et al., 2015), demonstrating that converged spaces have the potential to promote new repertoires of learning, literacy skills and high levels of on-task talk.

POWER SHIFTS AND SOCIO-CRITICAL NEGOTIATIONS

It was interesting to see how the children assumed and assigned power positions in such flexible ways throughout the study, sometimes situating themselves in more powerful positions as leaders and mentors, and at other times as followers and learners. Winters and her colleagues (2015) also discuss these types of stances in their research that clearly demonstrated how school children assume and assign authoritative subject positions (e.g., as directors, playwrights and performers) using digital cameras in order to build and participate in a play they were producing. By changing their stances in flexible ways, these older children were able to make decisions, interact with those around them and gain authority in order to control the action or save face when needed. Similarly, in our study with younger children, although they appeared less worried about authority positions, they did like to have opportunities to speak to one another and refute ideas (Vignette #5).

Vignette #5: Voicing Opinions

Two children were sitting at a table playing the Grandma's kitchen app on two separate iPads. At one point, Grandma, the app's central character, asked the user to 'Give Grandma a kiss'. Maverick, who was a leader in the class tapped the screen and moved on. Nadia however, did as she was instructed and kissed the iPad screen. This caused Maverick to react and to position her as being less aware. In a joking manner he stated, 'You don't have to kiss it. You just have to tap the screen.'

In the above vignette, it became clear that Nadia was less familiar with the app or at least the nuance of being able to tap the screen in order to move forward in the game. Seeing this, Maverick assumed a leadership role, instructing her on how to proceed. Conversely, on a subsequent observational visit, these same two children were again using the iPads side by side, playing a maze app that required them to move a marble through a maze by tilting the tablet. This time it was Nadia who showed the screen to Maverick and helped him to navigate the maze app. A few minutes later, he appeared more successful and succeeded at increasingly complex levels.

It was not uncommon for the children to demonstrate a fluid range of subject positions during the study. Here, the children moved in and out of social hierarchies – first positioning each other as experts/amateurs, then later as equals. According to Dyson (1997), 'Children have agency in the construction of their own imaginations' (p. 181). We saw agency during this study, the children made choices of their own will to invite help, refute ideas, be silent and take authoritative positions to satisfy their needs and to speak their thoughts. They navigated the social spaces they encountered in flexible ways, by simply adjusting a storyline or positioning someone differently. As time passed, we noticed even more flexible thinking, perhaps because the iPad users became: (1) less territorial about the tablets; (2) more familiar with the apps themselves; (3) more practiced as socio-critical negotiators; and (4) more invested in their own inquiries.

IMPLICATIONS FOR iPads IN SCHOOLS

As the *Crayons and iPads* study progressed, the children recognized that they would get a turn and they appeared less controlling. Some other strategies that were implemented throughout the study that seemed successful included: (a) ensuring that every child had opportunities to participate; (b) limiting the number of and types of apps available; (c) connecting the learning with the children's personal experiences and learning styles; (d) identifying the learners' interests; and (e) tailoring the children's needs to the apps themselves. The educators noted that after these changes were made the children were more willing to take risks and spend more time solving problems and producing creative work (as opposed to flitting in and out of apps and passively consuming). In this way, children were positioned as co-authors. The learners assumed these new roles in flexible ways and began to share their work more freely within the apps themselves, but also within the classrooms. Moreover, the positions of dominance subsided and partnerships emerged. Mrs. Walden mentioned that waiting to use an iPad was hard for some of the children, but they learned to consider the feelings of others by having to wait to use the device. She felt this was a good opportunity and offered authentic experiences for learners to develop empathy.

Furthermore, the educators agreed that the children got better at sharing and working together over time and with experience. Educators discussed that although they would introduce the tablets differently if they were to replicate the experience, the collaborative inquiries themselves were strengthened by the iPads (e.g., through use of the Internet, photography, video footage, voice recordings and the apps used) and the socio-critical negotiations that occurred throughout the process.

CONCLUSION

This chapter examined the ways young children collaborated and socially negotiated subject positions and power within an inquiry-based pedagogy, specifically when using iPads. Here through the use of vignettes, young children were shown to be interacting, refuting each other's ideas, dominating and helping each other while working with digital tablets and actual artefacts. The iPads offered a converged space, calling forth flexibility in children's positioning, agency, negotiations and collaborations with one another. The iPads appeared to invite shifts in power that were subtle and often playful (e.g., 'just tap the screen'). Though socio-critical interactions have long been explored within classrooms, including the ways that children participate together, negotiate social activities, assume perspectives and position others, the digital tablets added another dimension to this experience.

5

TABLETS AS INVITATIONAL SPACES

Leslie Memme and Kari-Lynn Winters

Abstract

Digital tablets can foster learning practices that are authentic, collaborative and creative. In this chapter, we again draw on illustrations and excerpts from the *Crayons and iPads* study to further our discussion introduced in the preceding chapter on the role of tablets within inquiry-based ECE classrooms. Findings demonstrate that while iPads afforded children opportunities to individualize their learning, build bridges between lived and virtual experiences and draw on personal backgrounds, there were also some challenges to be negotiated. Despite these hurdles, we highlight how iPads can be utilized as valuable invitational tools for children living and learning in the 21st century.

Keywords

iPads, Early Years, Digital Learning, 21st-Century Skills, Invitational Spaces, Provocations, Inquiry

WHY INCLUDE DIGITAL TOOLS IN ECE CLASSROOMS?

A variety of reasons might guide the decision for educators, administrators and researchers to recognize the necessity of incorporating tablets into ECE classrooms. First, children are using technology seamlessly in their own lives; a parallel of this type of thinking and mode of learning is advantageous within ECE. Second, ideas of authorship are changing; children need 21st-century competencies in order to participate in and collaborate with our evolving information economy (New London Group, 2000). Third, tablets provide opportunities to provoke and capture children's learning in authentic ways, as well as provide avenues to produce and share insights with others (e.g., snapping a photograph, creating a journal, video or multimedia presentation). Finally, not all children have the same access to information or technology (see Lane, this volume). Using tablets in schools can enable educators, administrators and researchers to meet the needs of some of our most vulnerable children. However, invitational spaces are needed in order to reach these goals.

WHAT IS AN INVITATIONAL SPACE?

Carla Rinaldi (2004), president of Reggio Children, focuses on sharing innovative pedagogies internationally with a diverse array of educators. She speaks about children coming to early education programmes as 'researchers'. Rinaldi asks questions such as: How can we foster a researcher attitude in children rather than giving them 'quick answers and our certainty'? And 'how should children be encouraged to take risks and construct their own theories while authentically working towards finding answers'? (p. 2). A priority for many educators is developing learning spaces where children can explore in these inquisitive and meaningful ways.

The learning environment in an ECE classroom is very influential on a young person's development (Carter, 2007; Ellis, 2004; Rasmussen, 2004; Strong-Wilson & Ellis, 2007; Wein, Coates, Keating & Bigelow, 2005). The physical environment has significant power to support an educator's pedagogy and children's learning (Ahrentzen & Evans, 1984; Lackney, 2008). The materials made available, the placement of furniture or the arrangement of centres facilitates or encourages certain types of play (Wein, 2008; Wein et al., 2005). Several scholars (Carter, 2007; Strong-Wilson & Ellis, 2007; Tarr, 2004) ask educators to think carefully about their classroom environments and to reflect on how the actual physical space is interpreted by young children. Tarr (2004) explains that a cluttered or 'busy' classroom can actually have a detrimental effect on children's learning. Conversely, a learning space that allows a child to feel like a creator – where they can manage and control their own space – offers 'new ways of thinking and working' (Goouch, 2008, p. 99).

The classroom environment is often referred to as the 'third teacher' (Strong-Wilson & Ellis, 2007). As Wien (2008) explains, this 'notion (of the environment as the third teacher) speaks to the capacity of the environment to engage and shape learning interactions' (p. 9). Rogers and Whittaker (2010) have looked extensively at classroom environments and have had multiple conversations with educators about creating an environment with this 'third teacher' idea in mind.

They focus on an invitational space – a space that invites investigation and wonderment where children can explore and discuss findings. Thus, educators must be intentional and make conscious decisions about the organization of the learning environment and consider how the space invites learning, investigating, exploring, creating and communicating (Chiarotto, 2011; Rogers & Whittaker, 2010). To extend this notion, this invitational space could also be what Gee (2004) refers to as an 'affinity space', where participants come together in one space to explore a common interest (e.g., cooking, building) and where students align themselves with others in order to learn from others in an apprentice/mentor arrangement.

PROVOCATIONS

Children are naturally curious, and a stimulating environment can help tap into and fuel this sense of wonder. 'Provocations' is a term used by early childhood educators to refer to items or ideas in a child's space that might provoke children to think creatively and ask questions (Harwood, Bajovic, Woloshyn, Di Cesare, Lane & Scott, 2015; Maloch & Horsey, 2013). Rogers and Whittaker (2010) discuss how they used an overhead projector to engage children in an exploration about shadows and light. These authors worked carefully with early childhood educators to 'create the environment as a third teacher' and 'provide an inspirational place for children' (p. 40).

The educators we observed in the *Crayons and iPads* study used multiple provocations, a combination of both concrete artefacts and digital offerings. One incidence that was particularly memorable occurred when a teacher brought a sewing machine into her classroom. The teacher was amazed by the inquisitive and insightful questions that were vocalized by the children after she simply placed it on a table in the room. Many of the children had not seen a sewing machine before and were very interested to learn how it worked. This began a series of questions and investigations using YouTube videos on the tablets to demonstrate the machine's functions and capabilities.

INQUIRY-BASED LEARNING

Inquiry-based learning is a pedagogical orientation common within many ECE programs. Based on a social constructivist view and the understanding that children create and construct knowledge from their social environment (Henderson & Yeow, 2012), this child-centred approach is fuelled by children's natural curiosity to make sense of their world (Chiarotto, 2011; Wang et al., 2010). Children engaged with inquiry-based learning are supported and guided while they ask questions, search for answers and co-construct knowledge with other learners who may be other children or adults (Atkinson, 2014; Harada & Yoshina, 2004; Pelo, 2006; Reiser, 2004; Wang et al., 2010). Educators often help children to formulate interesting questions, look for information, problem-solve, think critically, discuss and reflect on their findings (Atkinson, 2014; Chiarotto, 2011). Learning via inquiry is a process (Reiser, 2004; Wang et al., 2010) where children are challenged to think differently and to move past looking for simple answers (Atkinson, 2014).

CREATING AN INVITING LEARNING SPACE WITH iPads

Inherent features of an IPad such as sound, anImatlon, vIdeo, portablllty and a touchscreen interface seem to invite creativity. Within an ECE classroom, iPads can uniquely contribute to an inquiry-based approach. Inquiry-based learning spaces that include iPads are not only multimodal, they are often active, exploratory and collaborative. The ease to use iPad interface offers a feasible choice for classroom use, even for very young children (Melhuish & Falloon, 2010; Neumann & Neumann, 2014). Further, technology has the ability of 'extending the domain and range' of an inquiry (Wang et al., 2010, p. 381) and can also 'help learners succeed in more complex tasks than they could otherwise master' (Reiser, 2004, p. 273). Moreover, tablets are versatile, offer unlimited semiotic combinations of text, sound, animation, image and video, and appeal to males and females. In addition, tables are accessible to a variety of ages and appeal to learners with a range of interests and abilities (Neumann & Neumann, 2014).

Inquiry-based learning goes beyond simply asking questions. Rather, inquiry is the pursuit of understanding, sparked by an intrinsic curiosity and developed through a pedagogical orientation that is dynamic and emergent (Atkinson, 2014; Chiarotto, 2011; Pelo, 2006). In the *Crayons and iPads* study, inquiry foci were initiated in several ways. Sometimes children's own interests or experiences formed the bases for inquiry topics. For instance, the children in one classroom where we observed were particularly interested in music and instruments. The educator also had a keen interest in music and had recently started teaching the children how to play the guitar. Other instruments were available for the children to play as well. The children eagerly sought out song lyrics and videos on the iPads that were relevant to them. On multiple occasions and inspired by the movie *Frozen*, the children were observed singing and dancing. They knew most of the lyrics and were happy to demonstrate how they could play the music on the iPad while 'reading' the lyrics that the educator had printed for them. While listening to the lyrics from the songs, the children pointed to the words on their printouts, using mostly one-to-one matching, and when asked by the researcher to find specific words, such as 'bothered' on the page, they raced through the lyrics in their head to be the first one to point it out. The iPad was used as a complement to these developing inquiries as the children also recorded and replayed their song versions and dramatic enactments of *Frozen*.

Alternatively, at other times, the iPad apps acted as provocations and were used to explore subjects such as building, vehicles, cooking, music and drama. Building with Lego was a popular choice for many of the children in one particular classroom we studied. Recognizing this preference, the Lego app was introduced to the children. The app inspired some children to build with concrete Lego pieces while also building with virtual Lego within the app. The 'real' Lego creations were displayed with satisfaction in the vehicle museum set up by the children in the classroom.

Educators also initiated inquiries. For example, educators provoked explorations of nature, liquids and solids. Learning sometimes began in the classroom and then moved into another room in the school or outside to the playground. In the springtime, iPads were used outside to observe 'nature', enticing one child to ask, 'What is nature anyway?' Rather than simply providing an answer, the educator encouraged the children to use the iPads to explore and experience nature on the school playground. During this inquiry pursuit, children engaged in rich dialogue about 'what is nature anyway?' Further, they were able to document what nature looked like and sounded like from their perspective. The children recorded the sound of the birds, took pictures of the grass and the dandelions and created videos of the nature they observed around them. Even the youngest learners were seen working together to problem-solve, share ideas and explore.

CHILDREN CONNECTING THROUGH CONVERSATION ABOUT PERSONAL EXPERIENCES

Tablets also provide opportunities for children to connect their learning to their previous experiences. While creating a recipe in the *Grandma's Kitchen* app, one child, Wes, spoke to the researcher about the ingredients he was adding and the order in which the they needed to be added. At one point within the app, instructions are given to the user to put the ingredients into the bowl to make a cake. From the conversation that ensued while using the app, Wes demonstrated his knowledge of baking and previous experiences.

Wes: 'What do you need to put in first when you are making a cake?'

Researcher: 'I don't think there is an order.'

Wes: 'I like it to be in order.'

(*He pretended to put the milk in first.*)

Wes: 'Vanilla always goes last when mom and I are cooking. It's our secret ingredient. Vanilla always goes last.'

Though an iPad is not needed for a learner to connect their background experience to a classroom experience, the visceral nature of the movies within the app allowed Wes to see and replay the actual process. The directions for the recipe were both 'zoomed in' (e.g., a close-up shot) and step-by-step. The iPads afforded learners chances to practice and remember their past experiences or try something new, without educator direction or control.

iPads FOR 21ST-CENTURY LEARNING

The children in the two ECE classrooms we visited were excited by the numerous modes of representation offered by iPads and routinely engaged in these forms of learning. However, the importance of how iPads are introduced in the classroom became increasingly clear throughout the study. Many children had preconceived ideas about the tablet and wanted to use it to watch YouTube videos or movies. Other children vocalized preferences for specific games. In addition, the children we studied had various levels of ability in using the iPads or similar devices.

Educators wanted the children to view iPads as 'learning tools'. Our study demonstrated that these intentions needed to be made very clear to the children from the start. When the iPads were introduced to the children as devices for productivity and focused on inquiries, we found that children worked cooperatively together, creatively and demonstrated high-level thinking. The apps themselves were provocations for innovation and new ways of thinking. Similar to adding a mixing bowl and measuring spoons to the dramatic play centre, an app such as *Grandma's Kitchen* provoked children to think about and discuss the procedures used for baking, the necessity of measuring ingredients, and explain personal baking experiences (Figure 5.1).

iPads also provided opportunities for the children to learn about a range of inquiry topics. Some of the inquiries the children explored and examined during

Figure 5.1   Converged Play with Grandma's Kitchen app

our classroom visits included human development, Lego design and construction, pond studies, lifecycle of a tadpole, winter and ice, letters and numbers and colours. The tablets were used as research tools to inform children about their varied topics. In addition, the iPads were interactive and fostered collaboration, especially in relation to creating various multimodal products (e.g., videos, stories, voice recordings, scrapbooks, presentations). Children aptly combined varied types of media (e.g., sound, drawings, photographs, text, animation, video) to meet the needs of their inquiry pursuits. Educators felt that having all of these modes available in one device was a clear advantage.

Learning has undergone significant changes with various forms of technology, unlimited access to information, multiple social networking platforms and a rapidly changing job market impacting the skills needed by children in the 21st century (Barell, 2010; Dede, 2010; Fullan, 2013; Kay, 2010; Prensky, 2001). The foundations of these 21st-century skills are referred to as the 4Cs: communication, collaboration, critical thinking and creativity (Partnership for 21st Century Learning, 2015). The 4Cs were clearly evident in the observations of the two iPad-infused classrooms. Apps such as *iMovie*, *LEGO Movie Maker*, *Toontastic* and *Sock Puppets* sparked creativity, conversation and teamwork. While using these apps, the children produced original creations that were personal and unique to them. *iMovie* has a series of video editing capabilities that range from simple to complex, thus making it accessible for young children of all ability levels.

In one classroom, a few children had joined together to create a dramatized scene. When the researchers arrived with the iPads, they were eager to use the technology, equipped with *iMovie*, to capture their performance. Previously, the teacher had explained that if they recorded their piece, they would be able to watch it themselves and show it to as many other people as they wanted. These children quickly recognized that by using *iMovie* they could also edit, revise and retake the movie, improving their production. By using creative apps, the children began to see themselves as producers (Rowsell & Harwood, 2015). In fact, when using the *LEGO Movie Maker* app, users were directed to give their movie a title and to enter their own names as the producers. When the children replayed their production, they loved watching their name appear after the words 'produced by'. Children were often positioned as co-creators while using these types of apps. Children were observed taking pictures together, recording videos, discussing special effects and adding sound.

Similarly, digital storytelling apps such as *Toontastic* and *Puppet Pals* allowed children of varying ability to create short animated productions to accompany their inquiries. Children were directed to choose characters and settings while moving images around, adding dialogue and music. Some children worked together on iPads, discussing and collaborating on ideas. Often children on separate iPads were also working together. Comments such as 'Can you tell me how to find that?' 'How did you do that?' and 'Hey! Look at this!' were heard frequently. *Storybook Maker* inspired children to observe and discuss their environments, culture and thinking – ideas that they could also use in their books. Together they gathered materials from around the room and cooperated to create original stories. Here, children could write, take photos, use pictures from their own photo libraries, label the photos, add sound or assemble collages.

The iPads also appeared to invite children to work collaboratively to solve problems. In one case, a child was getting frustrated because she was trying to use the finger pinching motion to resize an image. When she asked for help, another child responded and sat with her. Together, they problem-solved, eventually discovering that for this particular app the pinching motion did not work and a different technique was developed for resizing images.

In addition, sustained opportunities for the 4Cs were evident. For example, one group of children enjoyed using the *Storybook Maker* app to take pictures of each other within the app, writing captions to describe their classroom experiences. Because of the unlimited opportunities offered by this app, children returned to this app in subsequent weeks, taking more pictures to add to their library or storybook. Moreover, they experimented with various templates each time they returned to this app. Finally, we observed the children discussing how they might continue working on their projects throughout the week. Children returned to these creative production apps and projects again and again – sometimes to complete them and other times to edit and improve upon them.

Conclusively, iPads can provide opportunities for children to share their videos, animations, storybooks and digital puppet shows through a variety of online channels. Possibilities include emailing, posting on a classroom blog, sharing on a classroom Facebook page or publicizing on YouTube. An option to disseminate work in a public digital library, through the app itself, was also available for some of these apps. Being able to circulate their work beyond the school walls gives children opportunities to experience a larger global audience and perhaps provoking new lines of inquiry.

CHALLENGES WITH iPads IN ECE CLASSROOMS

When learners are encouraged to be digital players, producers and explorers, encouraged to use the iPads creatively, thence the tablet's value as medium for learning can be realized. Indeed, in the two observed classrooms when the iPads were used with a clear purpose, and creative apps were coupled with generous amounts of time for experimentation, children demonstrated 21st-century thinking. Within this inquiry-based environment, questions were raised and knowledge was expressed in unique, differentiated ways. However, certain challenges also arose during our study. For instance, at times, educators were disappointed when children wanted to use the iPads to consume material (e.g., videos, music, images). Noticeably, children appeared passive and less interested in collaborations and provocations during these absorptive periods.

Security issues were also a challenge for the educators in this study. When looking at videos about how boats float, for example, side bar advertisements (popups) were inappropriate and became problematic. The unpredictability of the advertisements caused stress for the educators, and when popups were selected, these ads distracted learners. The educators in the study recognized and articulated that the affordances of the iPads made them worth the effort to find creative solutions to overcome these obstacles. Further, the educators experienced some frustrating connectivity issues that limited the availability of the Internet. Educators also struggled with a lack of availability of iPads within their school (i.e., the research iPads were the first prolonged exposure the classrooms had experienced). Lastly, the educators identified a strong need for continuous professional development opportunities to help them understand and capitalize upon all the benefits of iPads. A desire for further professional development opportunities for educators using iPads was found in other studies as well (Flewitt et al., 2014; Melhuish & Falloon, 2010).

IMPLICATIONS AND CONCLUSIONS

Several examples have been presented to demonstrate the multiple ways iPads were used within two ECE classrooms over a ten-month period. We observed iPads being used as invitational teaching tools that provoked children's inquiries, creativity, problem-solving, collaboration and communication – 21st-century skills. Further benefits of using iPads within ECE environments included connecting classrooms to the world, empowering children through individualized learning experiences and constructing opportunities for children to be both producers and consumers of texts. The mobility of the iPads extended the children's learning outside the physical classroom. When access was available, iPads were seamlessly integrated into these children's lives in authentic ways. The iPads also helped children associate past experiences with virtual understandings. The apps triggered meaningful conversations about their individual experiences, while challenging their current awareness and scaffolding deeper understandings. Hence, the children consumed knowledge (e.g., watching a video), while also creating, capturing and communicating their own ideas and feelings, often in collaboration with others.

Some of the challenges that we observed during this study included the logistics of bringing technology into learning spaces, advertisements, connectivity issues and iPad availability. In addition, some apps seemed to allow users to be passive consumers of information. Educators must carefully consider how iPads are accessed and shared. We noticed that when the children had consistent access for longer periods of time, they were more productive and eager to be digital explorers and inventors. Educators need in-service training to better understand the varied models of tablet integration as well as gain insight about the types of apps that lead to creativity and production as opposed to simple passive consumption. When this support is offered to educators, tablets become invitational teaching tools, capable of fostering inquiry and connecting children to the world around them.

6

'LET ME SHOW YOU HOW TO PLAY WITH THE iPad'

Young Children as Teachers

Debra Harwood and Katelyn Scott

Abstract

Several different terms have been used to describe the contemporary child phrases such as 'digital native' and 'millennial child'. As Zevenbergen (2007) points out, the contemporary child processes are vastly dissimilar as their thinking will be at *twitch speed*, processing thoughts in a parallel and connected fashion, often taking their cues from the graphics and visual representations first. These learners, possessing a robust *digital habitus* (Zevenbergen, 2007), will be digitally connected to others and active new medium learners with a view of 'technology as a friend' (p. 22). The potential difference between how young children and their educators view and use new mediums provides an opportunity to reconsider the teaching–learning relationships within ECE. In this chapter, we highlight specific iPad encounters from two different research projects and argue that the role of educators is a shared responsibility within the contemporary ECE classroom.

Keywords

Digital Habitus, Digital Natives, Converged Spaces, Child as Protagonist

DIGITAL HABITUS OF THE YOUNG CHILD

In 2001, Marc Prensky coined the term 'digital natives' in relation to the post-secondary students he was encountering – possibly not envisioning how the phrase might one day be applied to young children. But if we unpack the meaning behind this commonly used phrase, we can easily apply this terminology to describe the 5-year-old contemporary child. Children born in the 1990s and afterwards live in a world of access, use and exposure to new mediums; technology and information access is part of their worldview. We have encountered children as young as 3 years who readily understand the language of navigation, design, hyperlinks, multitouch and multitasking. And certainly, the pervasive force of social media is apparent among older children and youth populations (Mascheroni & Ólafsson, 2014). Often in the world outside of school, children and youth demonstrate competency and they are powerful contributors in shaping the world around them. Fandom accounts on Instagram, Snapchat or Wattpad show how children and youth engage in complex, creative and multifaceted digital practices, exercising agency to contribute to their own unique worlds while also helping to transform adult culture (Corsaro, 2011). Thus, children appear to be navigating and making meaning within the digital world well before their first day of formal schooling. Conversely, within more formal educational contexts, children experience what Yelland, Lee, O'Rourke and Harrison (2008) label as a 'heritage curriculum', a conservative and testing-focused school culture that places emphasis on fundamental 'back-to-the-basics' skill acquisition (e.g., reading, writing, mathematics). And although some educators want (and succeed) in finding ways to incorporate new technologies, the digital habitus (Zevenbergen, 2007) of children is distinct and needs to be recognized and appreciated.

Aptly, Zevenbergen (2007) borrows from the work of Bourdieu (1977, 1986) to theorize about the ways in which technology has shaped and influenced young digital natives *seeing* and *acting* in this world. Bourdieu (1977) sees power as culturally and symbolically created and constantly legitimized through the interplay of agency and structure. He argues that the main way this happens is through *habitus*, which can be understood as a system of lasting, transposable dispositions. These dispositions, which integrate past experiences, function at every moment as a strategy-generating principle, 'a matrix of perceptions, appreciations and actions' (p. 83), and enable individuals to cope with unforeseen and ever-changing situations. In this way, habitus may be defined as the embodiment of culture, providing a lens for our everyday thinking and acting.

Using this construct of habitus, Zevenbergen (2007) argues that growing up in a world rich with digital technology (i.e., digital natives; children) offers potential for a very different experience in constructing a digital habitus compared to those who have not (i.e., digital immigrants, adult educators), who instead reconstitute their understandings by adopting technology. While

Bourdieu (1977, 1986) focuses on social class habitus, noting that habitus tends to be common within social groups having similar life chances and life obstacles, and similar social, economic and political life trajectories, Zevenbergen (2007) reappropriates Bourdieu's work to allow for the construction of a digital habitus among young children. Here, we argue that Zevenbergen's (2007) construction of a digital habitus among younger people with computer technology (which allows for the theorization of particular dispositions towards the use of digital technologies) can be expanded to include iPads.

For young digital natives (i.e., children in ECE classrooms), ways of acting and being in the social world are framed by their experiences with technology. In turn, such experiences alter their dispositions to learning and behaving in ways that stand in contrast to their adult counterparts, the digital immigrant educator. In one research observation session, Katelyn was conversing with a child about the drawing she was creating on an iPad. Noticing that the 'ink' the child was colouring with was translucent (not opaque) so that the child was able to layer the various available colours on her electronic drawing over one another, Katelyn exclaimed, 'Wow! That's just like real colouring'. Looking up from her iPad with a puzzled expression, the child responded back, 'It *is* real colouring'. Similarly, at an alternate site, another incident further highlights this difference in worldview between the adult and child. One of our fellow researchers on the project decided to bring several small, hand-held toys to the research site for one of the visits, including an etch-a-sketch and a board game called Labyrinth. The first child to encounter the etch-a-sketch immediately asked how to turn it on, and 'is it a TV?' The adults in the room found the questions about the etch-a-sketch humorous. The educator commented on how 'funny' the question seemed since the toy itself was a common addition to the classroom in her early teaching years and certainly a part of her own childhood.

These examples help highlight the differences in dispositions towards technology and provide further support for Zevenbergen's (2007) notion of a unique *digital habitus* in young children, with arguably important implications for child educator conversations and interactions. So if young children are seen as holding a *digital habitus* that differs from their adult educators, the implications for practice within ECE seem profound. We ask: 'Who is the 21st-century child? What are the pedagogical considerations for educators that might result from these varied dispositions?'

WHO IS THE 21ST-CENTURY CHILD?

Whether we use the term 'digital natives' or 'millennial generation' (Howe & Strauss, 2000), what remains clear is that the contemporary child's life is 'digital and they communicate in a variety of modes with myriad materials that are made of bits and bytes' (Yelland et al., 2008, p. 2). Certainly, we are not suggesting more binaries (nature/culture binaries) (Taylor, 2013). And even the label 'old' or 'traditional' is problematic, but we will use it here for lack of a better descriptor. And without refuting the essential role of 'old technologies' (e.g., pens, crayons, books) (Yelland, 2011) or 'traditional play' (e.g., play with trucks, rough-and-tumble play, etc.) within children's lives, we see all of these resources and contexts as important mediums for children's play, learning and meaning-making. What strikes us as central and significant to the dialogue is exploring and understanding the ways in which children traverse, meld, create and transform these resources and contexts in new and unique ways when they communicate, interact, play and learn. By acknowledging the competence of the young child in this converged world (Edwards, 2013b), one also does not nullify the role of the educator.

Comparatively, the educator is an equally important *protagonist* in the child's learning journey (Rinaldi, 2006). As such, the educator must clearly understand the 21st-century child and act in ways that are supportive and intentional of children's multimodal capabilities (Harwood, 2014). This means first acknowledging the expertise of the child with new mediums and finding ways to counter the 'heritage curriculum' (Yelland et al., 2008, p. 1) that many children confront within early-years contexts. We see this 'heritage curriculum' as one that focuses on the teaching and learning of basic fundamental skills such as reading, writing and mathematics within a testing culture. As Kalantzis (2006) points out, a major shift has occurred that requires a 'rethinking of the nature of pedagogy' (p. 7). Hence, children are no longer satisfied with being *receivers* of information in learning contexts, where knowledge is transmitted anachronistically by the educator. Rather, we encourage educators to view children as powerful and knowledgeable agents in their own learning journey, a fact that must be recognized and mirrored within pedagogical practices.

As we spent time observing the 3- to 5-year-old children in their ECE classrooms, we were struck by their levels of knowledge. Many were well-versed in discussing things like streaming (from Netflix), purchasing and downloading apps (from the iTunes store). What's more, these young learners tended to be uninhibited when using the iPads we had introduced into their class or any of the apps for the first time. They were curious, adventurous and playful in navigating and operating the iPad. The children with access to iPads or tablets at home were well-versed in understanding the functions and capabilities of the devices, often acting as mentors for their more novice peers. Whether it was demonstrating how to take a photo, uploading a picture to the class folder in the photo stream or navigating levels of challenge within an app, the children tended to master these tasks quickly, enabling them to then teach their friends. Children were confident in disrupting typical classroom routines and reconfiguring spaces within these new digitally infused environments. In these ways, the children took on the role of teacher in the classroom, a role not all educators might be comfortable with or accustomed to.

Conversely, the educators we have encountered in our research projects have approached tablets more hesitantly and cautiously. As part of a separate study that examined early childhood educators' content knowledge and use of tablets within their classrooms (what we refer to as the CKS study), Katelyn and Debra (along with two other colleagues) offered a series of training sessions to 26 educators. As part of this project, we also provided continuous support via a blog and one-to-one tutoring as well as access to an educational technology specialist. The overall goal of the study focused on examining educators' self-reported beliefs regarding technology as well as investigating what iPad integration looked like in practice (Di Cesare, Harwood, Julien & Scott, 2015). These educators were asked to implement iPads within their classrooms, a novel experience for both the children and themselves. Quite perplexing was the level of encouragement the educators needed in the first three-hour training session to approach the device, some urging to remove their newly acquired tablet from its box. In general, we found the adults were more likely to 'ask first' before touching the new device. Moreover, throughout the study, the educators appeared to lack the intuitive sense of manipulating the basic functions of the tablets that we had so readily observed in young children in the *Crayons and iPads* study. And beyond this general hesitancy in approaching digital technologies, we also observed a level of uncertainty within educators' practices in finding ways to fully integrate technology despite the training and supports provided (Di Cesare et al., 2015). Educators' perceptions of the role of technology in children's lives impacted their integration of tablets within pedagogical practices. Moreover, these perceptions appeared to be persistent across the year-long study and somewhat resistant to change.

Admittedly, within our research projects, our sample sizes were small and comprised of very few educators working with new mediums within their ECE classrooms. Moreover, we have purposefully highlighted the differences between children and educators' digital habitus as a way of emphasizing the uniqueness of the 21st-century child. And beyond these differences in how adults and children negotiate these new mediums, as researchers we have come to accept that children play along a continuum of offline and online spaces (Marsh, 2010a) in what Edwards (2013b) describes as a converged play space. Edwards (2013b) adopts a post-industrial conceptualization of play that affords latitude for the diverse ways in which children today engage in play. Thus, play for the 21st-century child blurs the boundaries between real and virtual, traditional and digital (Edwards, 2013b; Marsh, 2010a; Plowman et al., 2012). Yet, this idea of 'convergence play' seems problematic for many (Bodrova & Leong, 2010), and digital play remains a 'contested activity' (Stephen & Plowman, 2014, p. 330) within ECE contexts.

THE 21ST-CENTURY CHILD'S CONVERGED PLAY SPACES

The contemporary child's world of converged play spaces may seem quite foreign to an early childhood educator who was most likely trained in the last century. Certainly, the debate on the role and appropriateness of digital world and the young child continues with some technophobic categorizations appearing in the literature (Edwards, 2013a; Frost, 2009). And despite the research on children's balanced usage of technology in their home environments (Plowman & Stevenson, 2012; Plowman et al., 2008, 2010) and the growing body of evidence on the depth and richness of play experiences afforded with new mediums (Marsh, 2010a), cautionary tales still persist within ECE (Cordes & Miller, 2000; Grimes & Shade, 2005). Like others (Black, 2010; Burke & Marsh, 2013; Marsh, 2010b), we think the idea of converged play spaces helps better account for the range of platforms, both traditional and digital, that children typically engage and enact within their play. And based on a definition of learning that focuses on the sociocultural context, perhaps as Marsh (2010b) suggests, play is better viewed as existing along a 'continuum in which children's online and offline experiences merge' (p. 25).

A striking example of this continuum from our *Crayons and iPads* research observations involved the multiple representations, transformations and ludic engagements that unfolded in relation to the Disney movie, *Frozen*. The movie *Frozen* made its debut late in the fall of 2013 and became somewhat of a worldwide phenomenon. In each of the five early childhood classrooms, we were to witness children playing, constructing, talking, writing, creating, drawing and dramatizing their own versions of *Frozen*. While we recognize that research on the role of digital technologies and 21st-century media is still unfolding, studies on the impact of television on children's play has a well-established history. Television has long been recognized as a source of both positive inspiration and negative influence on children's play (Singer & Singer, 2005). And Bishop and Curtis (2001) noted that children regularly make references to programme characters, imitated gestures, blended characters and plots from television within play.

In our observations of *Frozen*-inspired play, we noted children often referenced Elsa and Anna (two characters in the movie), copied or replicated some of their gestures, and at times closely replicated the storyline, while in other instances creativity prevailed (e.g., Elsa was paired with Snow White in a digitized story creation). These creative endeavours tended to be multimodal in nature, combining elements of concrete play (e.g., props, dolls, paper, and art materials), pretense and digital play (e.g., digital photos, audio recording, filming and digital story writing). What's more, these play experiences did exist along a continuum of online and offline settings (Marsh, 2011), settings that flouted both the present time and space context that the play unfolded within (Marsh & Bishop, 2014). In our examples here from *Frozen*, the children's play bridged their experiences from home, involved a multitude of mediums and implicated different players across the varied weeks as the play unfolded.

In her conceptualization of literacy learning, McTavish (2014) uses the phrase in-between spaces. She explains that as children negotiate their daily lives and social interactions within both formal and informal literacy contexts, they find ways of reconceptualizing those practices in 'flexible, playful and technologically contemporary ways' (p. 319). Here, we extend this concept of in-between spaces to help further our thinking about children's play and learning. Certainly, children's engagement with *Frozen* existed within this in-between space. Frozen theme-related play was evident in children's socio-dramatic activities, as well as embedded in various numeracy, creative arts, literacy and outdoor play pursuits. And although the educators were quick to capitalize upon the children's interests in 'everything related to Frozen', often finding ways of valuing the iPads and the spectrum of affordances inherent with the device was viewed as a challenge. Clearly, the children we observed appeared more at ease inhabiting these 'in-between' (and converged) spaces than their educators. In addition, the children did not delineate between play and learning, digital play and traditional play (Figure 6.1). Like others (Nilson, 2014), we have also observed children competently using apps such as *Grandma's Kitchen*, *Toca Boca Band* and *Pet Doctor* as a 'point of departure' (p. 31) for their in-between (converged) play. There existed a reciprocal and mutually interdependent relationship between play with the iPad and play within the concrete world. Notably, where one play episode started or left off was indiscernible.

The vignettes of data from these two studies point to a potential schism between children and their educators. And although the young children demonstrated an ability to move seamlessly between the digital and concrete, equally valuing a full spectrum of play and occupying those in-between spaces,

Figure 6.1   Dramatizing and filming of *Frozen*

educators appeared much more rigid in delineating among modes and valuing certain types of play over others. Perhaps, this is not all that surprising. The majority of educators in both studies were veterans with over 10 years of experience within ECE classrooms. Expectantly, the educator's training would have emphasized concepts such as developmentally appropriate practice (Copple, Bredekamp & National Association for the Education of Young Children, 2009), the role of concrete objects on child development and the importance of naturalized play (Dietze & Kashin, 2011). Much of ECE thought (curriculum and pedagogy) is predicated on constructivist learning theories (e.g., Bruner, 1977; Piaget, 2001, 2007; Vygotsky, 1962). Hence, curriculum and pedagogy is structured so that children can actively construct their own understandings of the world by engaging with materials and authentic problems, typically in encounters with others. Conversely, new mediums that offer digital spaces or converged contexts for this active construction infringe upon many educators' notions of naturalized play and learning.

But just thinking about the digital native entering an ECE context with their background of 'highly digitized out-of-centre' experiences and knowledge (Zevenbergen, 2007, p. 20) and an expectation of being able to access, inhabit and transform digital spaces within their class makes us question whether ECE classrooms and educators are *ready for children*. Expectantly, how an educator responds to this 21st-century child will be largely dependent on his/her image of that child as a protagonist. And perhaps by viewing the child as a protagonist in their own learning, educators and researchers alike can come to value *what matters* to children.

CHILD AS A PROTAGONIST

This view of the child as a protagonist in their own learning is a central tenant of a Reggio Emilia approach to learning and teaching (Rinaldi, 2006). Such a view honours and privileges children's meaning-making processes and capacities, processes metaphorically represented in Reggio's use of the phrase 'the hundred languages of children' (Edwards, Gandini & Forman, 1998). These visual and graphic tools (or languages) that are commonplace within this socio-constructivist approach are more accessible to young pre-writers and pre-readers. Thus, alongside these graphic tools, other media (e.g., digital cameras, video, audio recorders and, we argue, iPads and other new mediums) can be utilized in children's learning, representations and play.

In our research studies, we have encountered educators who shared powerful and positive images of the young child's capacities, albeit capabilities that required nurturing by an educator.

Much of what we have observed (in the five contexts in the *Crayons and iPads* study and 26 early childhood programs in the CKS study) can be described as 'learning through play' pedagogy (Ontario Ministry of Education, 2016). Though the majority of these participants shared powerful images of the child as a protagonist, when integrating iPad technology, educators often appeared either reluctant to scaffold children's learning or intervene in any way. Figure 6.2 depicts a fairly common scene that we observed in one study. When engaged with iPads, children typically clustered together and worked alongside one another in a type of 'joint activity'; noticeably absent was the educator who tended to opt out of the children's digital play. The interactivity between the educators and children that we had readily observed before iPads were introduced was markedly absent once the digital medium was introduced into the class.

Another group of researchers in Norway noted similar findings (Vangsnes, Gram Okland & Krumsvik, 2012). Vangsnes and her colleagues' case study of Norwegian kindergarten classrooms found that during children's gaming activities, educators were largely absent and uninvolved. This was despite Norway's policy directives that emphasize the role of digital mediums and computer

Figure 6.2 Children cluster and collaborate on iPads

games as being a daily part of the kindergarten curriculum. Like us, Vangsnes et al. also noted 'dissonance in the didactical situation' (p. 1146) in the use of educational computer games, that is, the child and educator each appeared to experience the medium in vastly different ways. The children engaged with computer games as a social activity and as play, whereas educators 'want to involve the child in the dialogue as a medium for learning' (p. 1146). Vangsnes and her colleagues were not surprised by this dissonance and attributed it to the educators' general lack of familiarity with gaming and the nature and structure of the computer game itself (i.e., competitive and goal-driven versus collaborative and constructivist orientation of the Norwegian ethos).

Although the majority of educators in both our studies held a view of the importance of technology in young children's lives, often these perceptions were tempered with cautionary concerns related to the age of the child, over-exposure to technology and/or technology detracting from other types of play and experiences. Digital game play (with apps) was predominantly perceived negatively, although it was less clear how educators defined one app as a game and another educational. Clearly, the educators we encountered also exemplified this 'didactic dissonance' that Vangsnes et al. (2012) discuss. The educators, if perceived and deemed to have an educational use, valued only specific apps. For example, an app such as Story Maker was appreciated by the educators for its ability to foster emergent literacy skills and the ways in which the app extended or mirrored traditional literacy learning. The children tended to appreciate a much more diverse array of applications and focused more on the levels of challenge and complexity, the diversity of the games within an app, and fun and enjoyment.

TEACHING AND LEARNING AS A SHARED RESPONSIBILITY

Evidently, a didactic dissonance is impacting the experiences of children and educators within early childhood classrooms in how new mediums are valued, perceived and used. McTavish (2014) observed 'as adults, we may grapple with how best to account for the choices we have to integrate this technology, but for young children born into this technological epoch, there may be no choice; it is simply a way of being' (p. 320). Zevenbergen (2007) argues that using a Bourdieuian framing to understand the changing demographics of early childhood classrooms 'enables the practitioner to see the child not only as a product of social circumstances (i.e., out-of-centre experiences), but also as shaping the pedagogy and curriculum' (p. 20), as habitus – in this case, digital habitus – is both shaped by certain social conditions and also shapes those conditions. But given the disparate digital habitus of children and educators and the didactic dissonance that is prevalent, how can pedagogies which view teaching and learning as a shared responsibility and value the child as a protagonist be enacted within early-years contexts?

As a beginning step, we suggest a reframing of the pedagogical landscape where teaching and learning are performed as a shared responsibility between protagonists. Although parents and other adults in a child's life are equally important protagonists, here we limit our discussion to the child and educator. Significant to this discussion is the idea that children's learning is impacted by the ways in which pedagogies are enacted and contextualized rather than a result of some device such as an iPad (Kucirkova, 2014). Accordingly, an emphasis on examining pedagogies that support children's learning should be appraised from the child's digital habitus. For example, an educator might discount game apps such as Angry Birds or Temple Run as frivolous, aggressive or not educational. However, from the child's perspective, he or she may be engaged in evaluating varied angles, forces and speeds as they play and have fun with this particular app. As researchers, we have observed complex role negotiations, language use and problem-solving among children as they engaged in playing apps such as Angry

Birds; questions about gender, power and popular culture while playing 'non-educational' apps were also evident.

Thus, an educator must be able to discern these teachable moments inherent within a game app and be ready to scaffold the child's learning. What is important here is that the child must be construed as a partner along-side the educator, an equally important, integral and competent partner. By doing so, the hierarchical relationship that typically exists in a classroom can be disrupted and new pedagogical spaces created within the horizontal relationship more characteristic of digital environments (Sørensen, Danielsen & Nielsen, 2007).

In this volume, Memme and Winters discuss the intersection between inquiry and iPads as one of these pedagogical spaces. And elsewhere, we have also considered the intersections between inquiry-based pedagogy and iPads as a means of honouring the knowledge and agency of the contemporary child (Harwood et al., 2014). In addition, within the classroom, educators need to ensure there is ample unstructured time and diversity in the choice of modes made available to young children. Opportunities to blend out-of-school interests within online and offline spaces (McTavish, 2014) is significant to ensuring classrooms are ready and relevant for young children (Yelland, 2011).

Certainly, this reframing of the educator–child relationship implicates needed changes to the ways in which early childhood educators are trained. Educator training must include a more comprehensive and thorough under-standing and experience with new mediums – mediums that children are knowledgeable about and engaged with in their everyday lives. Taken-for-granted dialogues and binaries that have historically impacted and shaped the field of ECE need to be disrupted to encourage and afford spaces for ideas such as digital habitus and converged play. The idea of converged play seems particularly significant in pedagogical reframing and, as Farman (2015) stated, 'the virtual is thus not a simulation, but is something that exists in an important dialogic relationship with the material world' (p. 8). In this volume, Rose and her colleagues help to deconstruct the nature–culture binary (Taylor, 2013) that appears so prevalent within education. We also foresee the need for descriptions of play as pedagogy to be inclusive of digital technological play as an avenue to ameliorating binaries within ECE.

Young children are knowledgeable and capable digital producers, con-sumers and inventors (Kjallander & Moinian, 2014; Rowsell & Harwood, 2014). Children actively make meaning with and through their engagements with digital mediums and digital play in productive and transformative ways.

Thus, the relationship between educator and child must be equal to provoke, ignite and excite learning and the myriad of play possibilities within the classroom. 'Let me show you how to play with the iPad' should be a space we are all willing and capable of inhabiting as researchers and educators alongside young children.

7

iPads FROM HOME TO SCHOOL

Exploring Digital Divides in Early Childhood Education

Laura Lane

Abstract

This chapter explores the concept of 'digital divides' within ECE. The digital divide debate focuses on the disparities that exist within society in terms of access to technology based on demographic status (Compaine, 2001). First-level digital divides are focused on access to digital technologies and infrastructure, while second-level divide concerns differences in skill, cultural, motivation and perception and how these factors shape the experiences with technologies (Selwyn, 2004; van Dijk, 2005). Despite educational systems' efforts to increase access through enhanced availability, use of technology has emerged as a complex site of analysis. In considering ways in which access and use are viewed and experienced by parents, teachers and children in the *Crayons and iPads* project, this chapter illustrates some of the potential effects and implications of *home-to-school iPad digital divides*.

Keywords

Digital Divides, Technological Access, Technological Use, Parental Involvement, Digital Contexts

INTRODUCTION

Digital technology has become an essential component of engaging with and interacting within almost every aspect of contemporary western society

(Selwyn & Facer, 2014). Recently, with advancements in cellular phones and tablet devices, technology has become mobile and well integrated with day-to-day activities (Haight, Quan-Haase & Corbett, 2014; Male & Burden, 2014; Selwyn & Facer, 2014). Mobile devices allow users to converse with others, determine weather forecasts, measure time, track health statistics, play games, access information, among many other activities. For children, technology may offer opportunities to expand literacies, communicate through a variety of media and navigate multiple text formats (Stephen & Plowman, 2003).

Sociocultural influences are important when considering the digital contexts within which children learn (Selwyn & Facer, 2014). Children are now described as the net-generation, a cohort with skills and learning styles that are radically different than their parents' generation because of ways digital technology has prevailed in their lives (Margaryan, Littlejohn & Voit, 2011). Harwood, in this volume, discusses how portable technologies are becoming increasingly popular and accessible. Children use devices such as smartphones, iPods and iPad/tablets regularly for lengthy periods of time each day. Even if really young children are not able to use such technologies independently, they often learn from indirect experiences through observing parents or siblings (Stephen et al., 2013).

Young children are immersed in a world filled with technology. Everywhere from restaurants to museums, children are making meaning of images, sounds, space and print on screens (Wohlwend, 2010; Wohlwend & Merchant, 2013). However, not all young children have the same access to technology. Differences in access to and use of technology create what is referred to as digital divides. This chapter explores first-level digital divides as related to access, second-level divides as related to use by educators and parents, and concludes by reconsidering ways to bridge these divides. Understandings of the potential role of digital divides are unpacked by drawing connections between current literature and the experiences of educators in the *Crayons and iPads* project.

SOCIOCULTURAL UNDERSTANDINGS OF TECHNOLOGY

Sociocultural perspectives of technology focus on the ways in which technology influences the world around us. Instead of narrowly focusing on the functions of technology, sociocultural perspectives consider the means through which technology shapes our day-to-day lives, including education (Male & Burden, 2014; O'Brien & Scharber, 2006). Often digital technology within education has been credited as changing learning landscapes by increasing access to a range of social connections, learning resources and communication methods (Selwyn & Facer, 2014). Having opportunities to engage meaningfully with digital technology may promote children's opportunities to participate in new forms of learning and help transcend social inequalities (Selwyn, 2004). However, not all children have equal access to technology and, as such, social inequities materialize. Despite increased access to digital technologies for some marginalized groups (Gonzales, 2016), Ragnedda and Muschert (2013) noted, 'today the biggest concern is not always concerning access, but the divide among information "haves" and "havenots", resulting from the ways in which people use the Internet' (p. 2). Thus, it is also important to understand the ways that access to and uses of technology may create or perpetuate inequalities for young children (Gonzales, 2016; Stephen & Plowman, 2003). Potentially, children who have access to technology in the early years may also have greater opportunity to develop multiple 21st-century literacy skills. In addition, technology can be used and supported quite differently by educators, families and children. Some of these inequalities were noted in the *Crayons and iPads* project as the researchers observed different access to and uses of iPads in classrooms and at homes.

Having regular and consistent access to iPads in classrooms affords children the opportunities to integrate technology with play and learning, fuelling educators to explore ways technology may be pedagogically amalgamated. Despite potential benefits of technological integration within early-years contexts, fears of technology infringing on important childhood social, emotional and cognitive development still exist (Stephen & Plowman, 2003). With new technologies becoming more prevalent, it is important to understand the way access (first-level divides) and use (second-level divides) perpetuate and remedy existing social inequalities.

FIRST-LEVEL DIVIDE: ACCESS TO TECHNOLOGICAL DEVICES AND THE INTERNET

The concept of the first-level digital divide emerged in the literature in the 1990s. Theorists and researchers noted concerns related to children having access to a computer both at home and within schools. Only schools, homes and community centres located in high-income areas with access to financial resources tended to provide computers for children's use (Attewell, 2001). Consequently, children's access to technology was related to the existing sociocultural inequalities inherent with geography, income, education, age, disability and culture (Armenta, Serrano, Cabrera & Conte, 2012). At the time, the Internet was not widely available and desktop computers were predominantly stationary devices accessible in some homes, a few school laboratories and quite uncommon within ECE classrooms.

Fears of technological ghettoization emerged as researchers and politicians began to worry that those from low-income, non-white families would experience graver inequalities as a result of this lack of access (Attewell, 2001; Natriello, 2001). In reaction to such fears, schools and community centres became an important focus point for technological integration in order to address this first-level digital divide (Attewell, 2001; Natriello, 2001). Over time, desktop computers became affordable and much more common in many homes and educational environments (Natriello, 2001). Although concerns persist regarding the ability of marginalized communities to maintain access to the Internet (Gonzales, 2014; Gonzales, Ems & Suri, 2014), overall access to technology itself has increased (Gonzales, 2016). However, the current shift away from computers and towards mobile technology (such as iPads and tablets) (Chen, Gallagher-Mackay & Kidder, 2014) means initiatives to increase access to technology in schools and early childhood classrooms has been renewed (Fallon, 2013). Thus, first-level divides are still prevalent.

Initiatives to increase access to technology are motivated by perspectives that learning in early childhood should connect with everyday learning and practices, experiences that are often infused with technology. In addition, some researchers argue that access to technology may improve young children's readiness for compulsory education and may offer children a variety of resources to engage with different forms of play and multiple literacies (McPake, Plowman & Stephen, 2013). Currently, 80% of Ontario principals claim that technology is introduced to children in kindergarten classrooms with most having access well before attending their first day of school (Chen et al., 2014). In the *Crayons and iPads* study, all of the five classrooms (three kindergarten classrooms located in two different schools and two early childhood classes in one community-based location) had dedicated computer stations with one to three desktop computers available for children to play basic literacy or numeracy-based games. Before the research team's involvement, access to mobile technologies was non-existent and few representations of 21st-century digital mobile learning were evident. The community-based early childhood classroom was located in a mid- to high socioeconomic status area. And although the classroom itself did not have any iPads, all the children had access to iPads at home and appeared well-versed with using the devices after they were first introduced into their classroom. One school, serving a low socioeconomic area, did not have access to iPads, and very few children engaged with the iPads when they were first introduced. Moreover, few of these children reported prior access or knowledge of iPads from their home experiences. Only one of the kindergarten classrooms had regular access to iPads that were shared within the school. The remaining four sites gained access after being loaned iPads via the research project. The school with access was located in a middle-class area, and children came with a range of experiences using iPads. As a result, first-level digital divides related to access to computers and mobile devices was prevalent in these ECE classrooms.

Access to Internet

Access to the Internet is crucial in maximizing the educational uses and benefits of mobile technologies. Increasingly, iPads and tablets are replacing computers with programmes downloaded from the Internet and children's creations stored on online accounts (Haight et al., 2014). In addition, much of the information we access as a society is no longer available through non-technological means (Armenta et al., 2012). And like access to computers and mobile devices, not all communities have high-speed Internet capabilities and not all classrooms have access to the Internet (Chen et al., 2014). Lack of access to the Internet may translate into missed opportunities to access a range of online resources or social connections (Armenta et al., 2012). In terms of ECE classrooms, this may mean that parents are not as informed of events or policies through communication platforms such as educator blogs and school websites. Moreover, lack of access might mean that children are not exploring digital forms of self-expression, creativity and communication (McPake et al., 2013).

Internet access both within and across Canadian communities differs greatly. Within communities, divides in connectivity can be related to sociocultural factors such as family income, education and culture. Importantly, those with relatively high family income, post-secondary levels of education or were Canadian-born, have the greatest access to the Internet. Similarly, public educational spaces may have limited or no access to the Internet depending on how educational funding and resources are allocated. Between communities, access to Internet may differ based on geographical location and population size (Selouani & Hamam, 2007). For example, few rural communities have high-speed Internet available to them given that the installation costs in small towns are more prohibitive versus large urban centres with a sizeable population base (Noce & McKeown, 2008). Northern Canada's landscape and geographic characteristics present additional technical challenges. Internet service providers must contend with installing

Internet lines that run through remote, mountainous, rocky, frozen tundra areas that have little existing infrastructure such as roads and electricity (Haight et al., 2014; Selouani & Hamam, 2007).

High-speed and wireless Internet is often necessary for accessing a range of multimedia content and optimize the use of iPads. For example, iPads cannot link easily to a hard-wired connection; they rely on high-speed wireless Internet to download the large files often associated with educational applications. In the *Crayons and iPads* study, only one site had consistent access to wireless Internet. Some of the participating sites were beginning to install wireless Internet for educator access; however, this was a slow process and contingent upon restrictive policies related to Internet safety. Participating teachers in the project had hoped the iPads would offer opportunities to access information and build upon inquiries that would otherwise be difficult to explore. Although the participating schools were located in small urban centres with community access to high-speed Internet, school policies related to firewalls and data encryption limited the wireless Internet in each of the classrooms.

SECOND-LEVEL DIVIDES: THE ROLE OF GATEKEEPERS

Following discussions regarding first-level digital divides, researchers began to reconsider and expand notions of digital divides beyond access to include an examination of the ways in which technologies are used (Haight et al., 2014). Second-level divides are considerate of the ways that technology is differently engaged based on sociocultural contexts (Amiel, 2006; Attewell, 2001; Haight et al., 2014; O'Brien & Scharber, 2006; Selwyn, 2004; van Dijk, 2005). Concerns regarding second-level divides arose as increasing rates of technological access led researchers, educators and parents to debate the ways in which (if at all) children should be exposed to technology in ECE (Plowman & McPake, 2013; Rose, Vittrup & Leveridge, 2013). These concerns are also focused on exploring how gender, race, culture and ability impact the ways children are encouraged or discouraged to use technology. As such, second-level divides may be much more difficult to identify and ameliorate.

Parents, teachers and schools are important gatekeepers for children's use of iPads as they often determine the ways children will engage with technology. These gatekeepers have different values and levels of experience regarding technology which may have a greater impact on children's learning than access alone (Selwyn, Potter & Cranmer, 2009). In some instances, technology may be heavily encouraged, discouraged or used with moderation – all of which have implications on children's technology use. Therefore, simply having a computer or iPad that connects to the Internet (i.e., addressing the first-level divide) does not guarantee benefits. Technology must be used in meaningful ways that contribute to children's learning within ECE contexts for true benefits to materialize (Amiel, 2006; Attewell, 2001).

Roles of Educators

Use of technology and access are equally important. Thus, educators must facilitate children's use of technology in ways that are relevant and/or empowering (O'Brien & Scharber, 2006). In ECE contexts, this means facilitating children's agency to use iPads to explore and engage with the world around them in creative and unique ways (Hatherly & Chapman, 2013). Children should be encouraged to use voice recordings, photography, video and creative applications such as Story Maker. Exploring, documenting and representing their interests can engage children with iPads as producers and inventors (Rowsell & Harwood, 2015).

Alongside my fellow researchers, I observed instances where children created stories that included elements of multimedia (Woloshyn, Grierson and Lane, this volume). Such opportunities were not solely contingent on access to the iPads, rather educators often provoked or encouraged children to use the iPads in very specific ways. These methods were connected to the educators' abilities to effectively integrate technology into classroom practices and a general perception of technology as an important tool for use within ECE contexts (Cviko, McKenney & Voogt, 2014; Hutchinson & Reinking, 2011). Importantly, educators who feel uncomfortable using technology or who lack a technological pedagogy may not effectively encourage iPad use within their classrooms (Hatherly & Chapman, 2013).

The educators I encountered had varied levels of 'comfort' with using technology with two educators self-reporting their level as a novice, one as a comfortable beginner, and one as an expert. Throughout the study, the novice adopted varied strategies in both her own learning and teaching. Such strategies included seeking support from her teaching partner, experimenting with apps and questioning the research team. Throughout, she demonstrated an eagerness to learn and a willingness to take risks within her pedagogy. Toward the end of the observations, the teacher reported more comfort in using the iPads in her practice and encouraged greater risk-taking with the children (e.g., outdoor filming and story creations).

Educators with positive perceptions towards technology are more likely to use technology in their classes as opposed to teachers who are concerned about their own technological skills (Cviko et al., 2014). In addition to skill, educator beliefs influence technology integration (Cviko et al., 2014). Thus, educators who conceive of technology as a support for children's learning are more likely to promote its use. In addition, the promotion of technology within ECE may also be facilitated by broader educational goals and community support (Hermans, Tondeur, van Braak & Valcke, 2008).

Roles of Parents

Interrelated parents' perceptions may also influence children's access and engagement with technology (Chen et al., 2014). While parents decide whether or not iPads are present in the home, like teachers, their beliefs about technology also govern the ways in which children use iPads (e.g., entertainment or education, amount of screen time and as a shared or solitary activity). Today, children are bombarded with media and technology throughout their day. As technology becomes socially pervasive, many parents are concerned that a child's social, emotional and cognitive development is at risk (Plowman et al., 2008). As a result, parents may be resistant to the presence and use of technology both in the home and within ECE classrooms.

The 20 parents that responded to the *Crayons and iPads* survey comprised varied socioeconomic ranks. Nineteen of those families reported access to mobile technology at home. Interestingly, most parents expressed concerns for technology's addictive allure and relayed worries related to overuse. As one parent responded, 'Most 4 year olds already spend too much time in front of a screen'. Overall, the parents reflected a strong desire for traditional types of play for their child, such as 'outdoor activities and social activities'. Parental concerns that technology did not support children's learning and well-roundedness were reflected in descriptors of childhood becoming 'techie and robotic'. One parent commented, 'I see many kids who do not talk or play to others but spend all their time in front of a computer or iPad. This should be discouraged'.

While these parents expressed concern about the amount of time their children spent with new technologies (e.g., iPads), many stated that it was important for children to know how to use new technologies for their future success. Specifically, one parent stated that daily playtime on the iPad should be limited to one hour within school. She commented, 'I don't want my son to become dependent on technology but it's a need to know how to use them nowadays'. Parents involved in this study voiced the importance of moderation as well as fears of technology being too influential for young children.

Parent perceptions of technology tend to shape the ways that children take up technology at home. This home use and knowledge does appear to impact and influence the ways in which children also take up technology in ECE classrooms. However, it is important to note that children do not learn how to use technology by engagement alone. Instead, children learn how to interact with iPads through their own observations of other family members and social contexts. For example, a child may observe their older sibling engaging with an iPad at home which may prepare them with an understanding of iPads prior to entering a technologically infused ECE classroom (Stephen, Stevenson & Adey, 2013). As such, it is important to understand the multiple contexts that children may directly or indirectly learn how to make meaning of and use iPad technology.

ADDRESSING THE 'DIVIDES' OF ACCESS AND USE

ECE contexts wishing to integrate new technologies into children's play and inquiry may circumvent or overcome first-level and second-level digital divides by adopting different strategies. For example, sharing devices among classrooms or throughout a school ensures greater access for a multitude of children (Ciampa & Gallagher, 2013). The very *mobile* nature of iPads means that classrooms are able to easily share. However, this basic level of access appears to remain an issue in terms of equity. For example, the five classrooms in the *Crayons and iPads* study had varied levels of opportunity to access iPads with some affording different granting opportunities or supportive school board purchases, while other sites were excluded from accessing technology beyond what was supplied by the research project itself.

The decreasing costs of digital technologies, especially mobile technologies, may increase the prevalence in ECE classrooms. This may also mean rethinking school policies related to Internet access (Male & Burden, 2014). Policies need to be revisited and reconsidered to address both safety concerns and issues of quality access to the Internet. Moreover, adults interested in integrating technology into children's lives may need supports to facilitate meaningful engagement. The participants in our study suggested providing opportunities for educators to participate in professional development and preparatory time to experiment with apps as ways to enhance their own comfort with integrating technology. In addition, these educators valued the easy access to technological support that was incumbent of the research project. Parents could also benefit from resources that support meaningful engagement of iPads at home. For example, teachers may recommend that parents download literacy apps that children are engaging with in early-years centres. Moreover, ECE classrooms can help address any digital divides that might exist by keeping parents informed about the ways children are using iPads in the classroom. Apps such as Google for Education, Buzzmob and Edmondo have been developed to facilitate connection and collaboration opportunities between educators and parents.

New technologies will continue to emerge in the field of each childhood education and shape the ways children engage with the world. In order to facilitate technological equity as these new technologies emerge, it is important to continually consider sociocultural factors that may impact access and use. In addition, it is important to consider that new technologies alone do not guarantee learning for all children (Falloon, 2013b). Although technology may have many benefits for learning, this learning may not take place without engaged and supportive parents and educators.

MEETING ALL THEIR NEEDS

Tablets and Diverse Learners

Dane Marco Di Cesare, Tara Kaczorowski
and Andrew I. Hashey

Abstract

While children are immersed in a world filled with a vast array of mobile technologies outside of schools, the use of technology within schools continues to be the subject of considerable debate. Struggling learners, including those with exceptionalities, stand to experience considerable advantages by using mobile technologies across various learning contexts. Highlighting current scholarship within the broader context of technology-infused learning, this chapter explores how educators might begin to conceptualize the integration of mobile technologies into their instruction through the Universal Design for Learning (UDL) framework. We also examine how the affordances of various technology tools have the potential to positively impact the learning experiences of children with exceptionalities. Lastly, we highlight important implementation considerations for educators preparing to infuse mobile technology tools within their instructional approaches.

Keywords

Children with Exceptionalities, Struggling Learners, Students with Disabilities, Affordances, Mobile Technologies, Educational Technology, iPads, Barriers

INTRODUCTION

Today, early childhood classrooms are comprised of diverse learners with unique needs. Children with exceptionalities (i.e., diverse learners with unique needs) make up approximately 5.8% of the preschool population in the United States (U.S. Department of Education, 2014) and 1.7% of the preschool population in Canada (Human Resources and Skills Development Canada, 2011). Exceptionalities may impact a child physically, academically and/or socially, and may include learning disabilities, communication disorders, autism spectrum disorders, sensory impairments, intellectual disabilities and physical disabilities. In North America, a majority of school-aged learners with exceptionalities attend mainstream schools and are educated within general education classrooms for at least some portion of the day (Human Resources and Skills Development Canada, 2011; U.S. Department of Education, 2014). Thus, educators need to be prepared to support the needs of all learners within the same classroom. Pedagogically, the incorporation of technology in the classroom opens up new possibilities for engaging all learners through flexible and dynamic learning interactions. This chapter will discuss the potential roles technology can serve in supporting the learning and development of children with exceptionalities within an inclusive classroom. By drawing on current research exploring the benefits of mobile technology on children's learning, as well as on scholarship investigating the impact of various assistive and instructional technologies, we aim to provide the reader with a forward-looking and empirically based examination of the vast potential these technologies hold for young children with exceptionalities. In addition, we include scenarios and findings from recent research involving children and iPads throughout the chapter to further substantiate our assertions.

TECHNOLOGY FOR LEARNERS WITH EXCEPTIONALITIES

The use of technology to support the needs of learners with exceptionalities has traditionally been in the form of assistive technology (AT). U.S. federal law defines AT as 'any item, piece of equipment, or product system, whether acquired commercially, modified, or customized, that is used to increase, maintain, or improve functional capabilities of individuals with disabilities' (Assistive Technology Act, 2004). This form of technology is provided to learners based on their individual needs, enabling access to curriculum content or learning experiences that may otherwise be limited as a result of the disability. For example, an AT device might include the use of large print text for a child with visual impairment (e.g., an iPad or Kindle) or closed captioning to support a child with hearing impairment. For children with learning or behavioural disabilities, appropriate AT devices and services may not be as apparent. For example, a child with a learning disability may have limitations with his or her cognitive processing and working memory (Johnson, Humphrey, Mellard, Woods & Swanson, 2010), which could make it difficult to recall basic math facts. A learner with a difficulty such as this might use a multiplication table or a calculator for complex word problems to help him or her focus on problem-solving while circumventing the barriers posed by their inability to recall basic math facts. AT encompasses a broad range of technology applications and includes devices as well as services. One unifying aspect of all AT is that the devices provide individualized assistance and support to promote more equitable access to learning and thereby levels the playing field for children with exceptionalities.

In the United States, schools are required to provide appropriate AT services and devices to 'increase, maintain, or improve functional capabilities of individuals with disabilities' (Assistive Technology Act, 2004). These devices may also be provided for infants, toddlers and preschool-aged children as part of early intervention services in the United States, and the early intervention system of services is mandated by law in every state and territory (Individuals with Disabilities Education Act, 2004). Other countries have adopted similar practices. In Canada, some provinces (e.g., Ontario, Alberta) have government-initiated strategies in place to assist children with exceptionalities (and their families) to receive supports and services (Home Care Ontario, 2015).

As technology tools and applications continue to proliferate across all sectors of our society, the types of educational technologies available for use in schools today have become more mobile and flexible, offering educators multiple ways to address children's unique learning needs. Until somewhat recently in the United States, there were few processes by which schools or teachers could begin thinking about using digital technology with children, and most often this type of planning occurred strictly during the development of a child's Individualized Education Program (IEP). During this process, professionals comprising the IEP team collaborate to determine whether providing the child with AT would be beneficial. This process has represented a rather narrow avenue by which technology offerings can be thoughtfully considered (i.e., on a case-by-case basis). Today, however, multiple frameworks exist to help educators consider, select and implement technology in effective ways for a wide range of learners. Dominant among these frameworks is the concept of Universal Design for Learning (UDL, which can guide educators in designing curricula and educational materials to maximize children's accessibility while minimizing barriers to learning, including those barriers manifested by any disability.

TECHNOLOGY AND UDL

The term 'Universal Design for Learning' refers to an evidence-based framework for guiding educational practices and curriculum design which maximize the learning potential of the widest possible range of children. Although the framework has been continually refined over the past three decades, the three guiding principles have remained unchanged: to provide multiple means of (a) engagement, (b) representation and (c) action and expression (Meyer, Rose & Gordon, 2014). These principles can help educators move beyond the current paradigm of knowledge acquisition and towards developing the strategic learning potential of each individual child. The following explanations and examples of each principle are derived from the UDL guidelines developed by CAST, Inc. – an invaluable resource for educators seeking clear guidance about how to implement the UDL framework in their classrooms (Meyer et al., 2014).

The first principle of UDL, providing multiple means of engagement, prioritizes the unique role engagement plays in all learning endeavours. Motivation plays an especially critical role when children encounter challenging tasks, helping them to persevere when they might otherwise give up. Some of the ways in which teachers might enact this principle include providing children with options to recruit their interests (e.g., offering choice, supporting autonomy and enhancing the authenticity of tasks) or providing options to sustain effort and persistence (e.g., heighten salience of goals and varying demands and resources to provide optimal challenge). By attending to these affective dimensions that are so central to engagement, teachers can best ensure that children will approach their learning with eagerness and passion.

The second principle provides multiple means of action and expression and is rooted in the reality that learners should have many options by which to demonstrate what they know and what they can do. Conversely, when educators unnecessarily restrict the means by which children can express themselves in a learning context, we risk underestimating a child's knowledge or skills. These narrowed ways in which teachers may have sanctioned children's participation may represent a barrier (e.g., an oral report for a child with speech impediment). In order to foster goal-directed and strategic learning, children with widely varying skills and abilities should be provided with multiple options for expression and communication (e.g., leveraging media to communicate, using digital tools for composition, capitalizing on scaffolds to increase their transition to independence).

The third principal, providing multiple means of representation, guides us to think about the ways in which we can support learners' access to knowledge and understanding. To accomplish this, educators can provide options for comprehension by highlighting critical features, patterns and relationships in the content they teach. They can ensure children have the requisite background knowledge to be successful and help guide how they process and integrate new information. Another way to enact this principle is to provide children with options for how they perceive information. This could entail modifying or customizing how information is displayed or by providing alternatives to either auditory information or visual information. Shifting the focus to how educators can best convey ideas and information to children with different strengths, needs and preferences can help avoid the dangerous assumption that all learners should learn in the same way.

Recent brain research continues to affirm the variability of learners' brains as constant, predictable and distributed (Meyer et al., 2014). In other words, as educators, we should expect our children to present a wide range of abilities and needs and must consider this variability when designing educational curricula and materials. By designing flexible curricula and materials, educators become well positioned to help children reduce barriers to their successful learning experiences and therefore bolster their learning potential.

The notion of learner variability also has strong implications for how we think about children with exceptionalities. The UDL framework can serve as a means by which to re-examine the dominant perspectives on disability, which have historically positioned disability as residing within the individual (Meyer et al., 2014). In contrast, this framework prompts us to consider the ways in which our schools, curricula and educational materials might instead be the elements posing the greatest barriers to children's learning and success (Rose & Meyer, 2002). When observing children with exceptionalities learning in technology-rich, UDL-influenced environments, most strikingly we have noted how perseverance and achievement can be greatly strengthened with in-time supports made readily available to children.

Examining the role of technology within a UDL framework, intuitively one can see how technology could afford educators a diverse array of options for inviting and provoking learning within an inclusive early-years context. Generally, technology-infused curricula offer learners and educators with varied means by which to express and perceive information, engaging learners' attention and motivation and offering choice. While technology implemented as AT is directly tied to an individual learner's educational needs, instructional technology and supports implemented from a UDL perspective aim to reduce barriers to learning by offering learners multiple pathways (Rose & Meyer, 2002). Despite the differing orientations between AT and UDL, they share the primary goal of reducing barriers and increasing children's access to learning; this is perhaps why Rose, Hasselbring, Stahl and Zabala (2005) describe AT and UDL as representing 'two sides of the same coin' (p. 507). Although both share common goals, by nature AT is implemented on a case-by-case basis, while UDL provides an opportunity to incorporate technology to address the wide range of children's strengths and challenges in a way that maximizes success while minimizing barriers. A more thorough exploration of the unique affordances of ubiquitous mobile technology is, therefore, warranted to uncover the ways in which these flexible tools specifically can be leveraged to enhance learning opportunities for *all learners*.

Technology tools make it possible for both teachers and learners to use multiple modes (e.g., pictorial, video, aural, textual) to interpret ideas and express them to others. As Rowsell points out in Chapter 2, researchers adopting a multimodal perspective can broaden their analysis of how children understand, use and learn through technology tools. By striving to understand the relationship between a learning context, a user and the tools through which learning may occur, we can begin to think more critically about how the multiple modalities inherent with mobile technologies might offer distinct advantages for children to understand, act and engage within a learning context. When educators increase opportunities for children to use the full range of modalities to express themselves and simultaneously represent information and ideas with a variety of modalities, we also expand the possibilities for expression, representation and avenues through which teachers can engage learners.

INSTRUCTIONAL TECHNOLOGY

Though there are many accepted definitions, educational or instructional technology (IT) is generally referred to as 'the study and ethical practice of facilitating learning and improving performance by creating, using, and managing appropriate technological processes and resources' (Januszewski & Molenda, 2008, p. 1). While increasing numbers of educators are sure to integrate technology into their practice, it is still most often used for rather low-level activities such as lesson planning, information gathering and presenting, and grading (Gray, Thomas, Lewis & Tice, 2010). Among ECE professionals, the role of technology in children's learning is still greatly debated with polarizations appearing in the literature. Some scholars believe technology is detrimental to child development (e.g., Armstrong & Casement, 2000; Cordes & Miller, 2000; Radich, 2013), whereas others herald its benefits (e.g., Clements & Sarama, 2003; Plowman & McPake, 2013; Yelland, 2011). Ultimately, the usefulness of any pedagogical approach or tool rests on the *contexts* and *purposes* for which it is employed and, more importantly, on the impact it has on the learner and environment. As professionals who have worked in technology-infused classrooms as well as research settings, we have seen first-hand the power of technology tools to augment evidence-based teaching and learning approaches. But as with any tool, success hinges on the manner in which these tools are used.

Educators must be prepared and willing to let technology alter their instructional habits. All learners are able to construct knowledge with guidance and scaffolds. But learners need tools that are complementary to the instructional approaches used within their classrooms and throughout the varied learning experiences. Beishuizen (2011) reminds us 'the principal role of educators in a technology enriched learning environment [, therefore,] is establishing a balance between structure and freedom to learn in self-regulated way' (p. 120). Labbo and Reinking (1999) recommend that the integration of technology should be accessible to all learners, enhance instructional practices and prepare learners for the modern digital age. As educational technology has evolved and become more mobile, new possibilities for instruction are available, particularly when placed directly in the hands of learners.

Despite the increasing use of mobile technology in classrooms, there is a paucity of rigorous studies related to academic achievement and mobile technology (Penuel, 2006). Many researchers of mobile technology in the classroom still focus on measures of child engagement, qualitative anecdotes and perceived achievement (Wu et al., 2012). Children who use mobile technology for learning are often more engaged and interested in the lesson content – the first step towards making academic gains (Hlodan, 2010). The body of research involving mobile technology and children with exceptionalities is also quite limited. In a large meta-analysis of mobile technology research by Wu and colleagues (2012), only 0.56% of the participants included in the original studies were identified as learners with exceptionalities. There have been some recent studies examining the effects of mobile technology on outcomes for learners with exceptionalities, but most do not concentrate on learning specifically; instead, the research tends to focus on communication and behaviour (Kagohara et al., 2013). Albeit one study has examined academic outcomes for children with learning disabilities using computer-aided instruction, most of this technology was used as supplemental instruction (Seo & Bryant, 2009). Other research has focused on the effects of a single specific application on a mobile device (Fernández-López, Rodríguez-Fórtiz, Rodríguez-Almendros & Martínez-Segura, 2013). To date, no studies have focused specifically on the device with all of its affordances. Though more rigorous research is warranted to explore the impact of mobile technology on learning for children with diverse disabilities, the theoretical underpinnings are sufficient to support its use in diverse, inclusive classrooms. Mobile technology provides an avenue for learners to capitalize on the benefits of technology during instruction, particularly when it is paired with effective instructional practices.

INSTRUCTING WITH TECHNOLOGY TO MEET THE NEEDS OF ALL

Importantly, learners need freedom and encouragement to explore technology by themselves. As digital natives (Prensky, 2001), children's ability to find solutions should be valued and their digital expertise respected, if educators are to meet the needs of all children. Unfortunately, for many learners with disabilities, this is seldom the case (Di Cesare, 2015; Hashey, 2015). Both Di Cesare and Hashey in separate studies with middle and high school learners with exceptionalities found that participants reported rarely using technology in their classrooms. While a select few participants indicated they were occasionally permitted to troubleshoot classroom technology problems (i.e., fixing digital projector), most others reported being thwarted by either classroom educators or by the technology-restrictive policies in place at the school or district level. Research involving younger children echo these findings. Though many teachers have access to computers, either in the classroom or in a school computer lab, they are often underutilized (Cuban, 2009). By providing ample opportunities for learners with exceptionalities to explore and expand the ways in which they might access information or express their knowledge, educators can best support each child's learning and development.

While learners should be offered opportunities to explore technology and independently apply technology to their everyday learning, children should also be guided and supported through specific applications of the technology for learning. This aspect of guidance and support is particularly important for learners with exceptionalities. Kaczorowski (2015) found children with disabilities were shown to minimally improve their accuracy and independence in solving math equations and word problems when provided access to technological supports; however, they did not make the same kinds of gains as their peers without disabilities. Interestingly, Kaczorowksi found that when provided explicit modelling of how to use specific technological supports, all learners, including those with exceptionalities, were able to use the supports effectively and independently. The use of explicit instruction has been found to positively impact children of all ages (Archer & Hughes, 2010) and can be used to support children in acquiring knowledge of technology used for both assistive and instructional purposes. This underscores a critical – and perhaps underaddressed – issue in the literature exploring technology integration and learners with exceptionalities. In order for learners with disabilities to capitalize on the myriad affordances offered by today's technology, educators must be prepared to explicitly teach learners how to use the features of a technology device.

Explicit instruction is one pathway to ensure that learners overcome barriers they may face without the use of such a device. Tangentially, educators must be willing to explore the available technologies to such an extent that they can assess whether and how a device could be employed. A discussion on the various factors influencing educators' willingness or tendency to embrace teaching with technology is beyond the scope of this chapter, but scholars have engaged in a lively debate on the potential of technologies to enhance education, particularly whether it has a place in the early-years classroom. When districts, schools and classrooms embrace the presence and utility of such technologies, many evidence-based practices that have proven successful for learners with disabilities can be explored further (Kim, Vaughn, Wanzek & Shangjin Wei, 2004; Archer & Hughes, 2010; Cavanaugh, 2013; Hattie & Timperley, 2007; Haydon, Macsuga-Gage, Simonsen & Hawkins, 2012).

Evidence-based practices, such as Explicit Instruction (EI; Archer & Hughes, 2010), frequent opportunities to respond (OTR; Haydon et al., 2012), providing immediate feedback (both corrective and positive) to learners (Hattie & Timperley, 2007), utilizing specific positive praise (Cavanaugh, 2013) and providing multiple/multimedia representations of content with graphic organizers (Kim, Vaughn, Wanzek & Shangjin Wei, 2004) have all demonstrated positive impacts on the academic performance of children with exceptionalities. These impacts could be enhanced by the use of technology, yet there is often a general lack of specialized instruction for learners with disabilities (Zigmond, Kloo & Volonino, 2009). Further, the partnerships between classroom educators and special educators within collaborative co-teaching settings have long been the subject of debate (e.g., Baker & Zigmond, 1990). Co-teaching arrangements also present special challenges to teams in part because of the differing knowledge foundations and roles associated with classroom-based and special education teachers (Friend, Cook, Hurley-Chamberlain & Shamberger, 2010), with special educators often serving in supporting roles assisting the general education teacher instead of serving as instructional experts in the classroom.

Within inclusive learning environments, where co-teaching teams fail to capitalize on the respective and often complementary strengths of each partner (i.e., classroom educators' content expertise paired with special educators' instructional expertise), it is perhaps not surprising that blanket accommodations are provided for struggling learners and those with exceptionalities rather than carefully considering the specific needs of individual learners (Zigmond et al., 2009). While the UDL principles are also well suited to assist teachers in meeting children's diverse learning needs, they should work in tandem with the individualized accommodations deemed necessary by informed professionals. Whether assistive or instructional technology tools can serve an important role in addressing teachers' responsibility to deliver the optimal learning supports for all children, including those with exceptionalities? Fortunately, the unique affordances associated with mobile technologies can aid struggling learners by (a) leveraging portability and interoperability, (b) circumventing barriers related to fine motor control, (c) facilitating self-regulatory behaviours, (d) enhancing motivation and persistence and (e) increasing opportunities to provide immediate feedback.

AFFORDANCES OF MOBILE TECHNOLOGY

Many of the benefits of mobile devices are inherent in their design. These devices are portable, flexible, adaptable and accessible, which may allow exceptional learners to engage with the same activities as their peers (Chai, Vail & Ayres, 2015). Consider the non-verbal learner with significant communication needs. Specialized communication devices cost around $8,000 (Perez, 2013), but with universal mobile technology like the iPad, applications with similar functionality can be embedded as a socially valid learning tool at a fraction of the cost. Learners with exceptionalities who may not have the fine motor skills to work with a pencil or stylus are still able to fully utilize mobile devices through the use of Bluetooth-operated switch interfaces. Furthermore, the assistive touch accessibility feature on the iPad allows children with limited fine motor control full access to the device by exchanging multitouch gestures for on-screen button presses. Increasingly, developers are making their learning applications compatible with these built-in accessibility features like zoom, large text, colour inversion, voiceover and closed captioning (Perez, 2013). This allows educators to customize and adapt both application and content, thus meeting the needs of learners with exceptionalities (Chung & do Prado Leite, 2009).

In addition to the increased access to content, the portable nature of these devices promotes freedom of movement between different physical locations in and around a school, affording learners with exceptionalities to have access to the device in multiple environments. This can result in increased ownership and independence among learners with and without exceptionalities. In an exploratory study of elementary-aged children with and without exceptionalities, Kaczorowski (2015) found that access to mobile technology during independent math practice resulted in decreased reliance on teacher assistance and increased self-regulatory work habits. Rowe and Rafferty (2013) suggest with proper considerations that multimedia technology can actually assuage self-regulatory challenges of planning, knowledge activation, metacognitive monitoring and reflection when learning with hypermedia. Relatedly, Ciampa and Gallagher (2013) demonstrated how the incorporation of choice, immediate feedback, challenge, collaboration and competition on a mobile platform increased learner motivation and engagement.

With increased engagement comes more opportunity for learners to learn and engage with the material. Di Cesare (2015) found that exceptional learners who were characterized by inattention, disruption, frequent absences and low productivity expressed a desire to think critically and produce when given the option to use mobile technology with multimodal composing outlets. In Ciampa and Gallagher's (2013) study of mobile technology usage in an Ontario elementary school, teachers reported increased focus, determination and self-directed learning among children who utilized mobile technology in the classroom. Persistence and sustained engagement is particularly important for learners with exceptionalities. When provided with more opportunities to respond, learners with disabilities (especially those with emotional and behavioural disabilities) tend to increase correct responses and decrease disruptive behaviours (Sutherland, Alder & Gunter, 2003). The teachers in Ciampa and Gallagher's (2013) study believed the incorporation of mobile technology fostered the inclusion of learners with exceptionalities. One teacher explained how the struggling learners 'really come alive and shine when they can just do it on the iPod Touches and no one has to see what they are doing except for me and everyone feels successful because no matter what, you are having fun' (Ciampa & Gallagher, 2013, p. 319).

Meaningful utilization of mobile technology can also assist learners with disabilities in broadening foundational skills in a variety of academic areas (i.e., emergent reading, early writing and numeracy). A variety of the built-in accessibility features and applications on mobile devices can be utilized to assist learners with exceptionalities. For example, features such as text-to-speech, dictation, word prediction and autocorrect facilitate lower-order concerns (i.e., mechanics, syntax, spelling) and have been clearly identified in research as being beneficial for learners with disabilities, having positive impact on word production and compositional quality (Cullen, Richards & Frank, 2009; Evans, 2005; Garrett et al., 2011; Silió & Barbetta, 2010; Troia, 2006). In addition, the frustrations associated with paper and pencil materials (e.g., erasure marks, difficulty with letter/number sizing and spacing, spelling) can be alleviated with the features and capabilities of mobile devices. Here, features such as undo buttons, resizing tools, typed text, spellcheck can be particularly significant for children with exceptionalities as it is easier to move/manipulate digital text quickly and easily identify errors in spelling (Di Cesare, 2015). Further, children have demonstrated a higher tolerance for utilizing mobile technology and appear to persist through what adults may perceive as difficulties (Di Cesare, 2015; Kaczorowski, 2015). In fact, mobile devices can also function as sources of comfort when children are anxious. In the *Crayons and iPads* study, one of the children used the iPad as a calming activity. When he experienced anxiety or distress, the child requested to draw, but after the introduction of the tablets, he often augmented that request with the additional use of an iPad.

Applications and activities on mobile devices often include built-in opportunities for immediate feedback. For learners with disabilities, immediate feedback is an especially important part of the learning process (Archer & Hughes, 2010). Providing immediate corrective and affirmative feedback scaffolds the learning process by helping learners focus on accurate, essential content. Immediate feedback provided by technology is another avenue and asset towards building children's self-regulation, a key aspect of learning (Kaczorowski, 2015). Further, immediate feedback has implications for engagement in that the feedback can encourage perseverance when a child is faced with difficult problems, unlike pencil-and-paper activities where the feedback is not immediate (Ciampa & Gallagher, 2013; Di Cesare, 2015; Kaczorowski, 2015). The ability to include immediate feedback is important to consider when selecting assistive and instructional technology tools for 21st-century classrooms.

CONSIDERATIONS FOR MOBILE TECHNOLOGY IMPLEMENTATION

When implementing mobile technology, careful consideration must be taken to ensure the selected devices and apps complement AT devices and services. Many AT devices, such as special keyboards, switches, refreshable Braille displays and speakers/earphones, rely on Bluetooth capability in order to link to mobile devices. While all iterations of the iPad contain Bluetooth functionality, there are other brands of tablets that do not have this functionality. Consequently, it is vital to consider the capabilities of the devices used in the classroom, particularly if AT devices must be used in conjunction with the mobile technology.

Educators must also take care to ensure accessibility features and services either built in to the mobile devices or connected via other means (i.e., selectable text for screen reading, picture descriptions for images) work appropriately with selected apps. For example, if a child requires screen reading capability on a mobile device, an educator needs to ensure they do not select apps with text that is not compatible with screen reading. Not all apps utilize selectable text, and it is important to identify these apps before they are selected, particularly if a cost is associated with the app. A feature such as picture descriptions of images is another important consideration. Picture descriptions allow refreshable Braille displays and other devices to 'read' on-screen images. While an educator's classroom may not currently include learners who need such services, it is important to consider the needs of a diverse array of both current and future learners.

Young children with disabilities can and do learn to use mobile devices with very little instruction, although children with learning needs may require some additional explicit instruction or specific learning strategies when using mobile technology. In a pilot study conducted by Hashey (2014), middle school-aged children with emotional and behavioural disorders used the Notability app to compose argumentative essays on iPads. During an exploratory phase early in this study, participants used the Notability app to plan and compose essays, where they had many options by which to organize and write their notes and essays. Initially, learners' fascination with the stylus pens (one of several options to input text) led them to use this method of text entry instead of the keyboard. Notably, the children did fail to make use of other text annotation features capable of supporting their planning and revision behaviours. A simple keyboard can address any challenges a child might experience with writing legibility with a pen or pencil. And in this study, the allure and novelty of the stylus pen did distract the children's attention away from some of the more critically supportive features inherent to the word processor programs (e.g., legible fonts, spell checking capability).

However, after an orientation session where learners were explicitly taught how and when to use select features, along with a rationale for the options, the middle school children reported increased confidence in their ability and willingness to type their compositions. After this orientation, learners were taught a persuasive writing strategy and became increasingly aware of the value of the features they had initially overlooked. This excerpt from the research project does help to highlight the potential need for educators to allow ample time for students to explore technological features while also explicitly teaching children how to use all the inherent features of a digital tool.

Young children continue to engage with these complex technologies, and this scenario points to the value of affording learners the opportunity and impetus to think critically about how, when, where and why they might select one feature over another, thereby augmenting their ability to self-regulate their use of these powerful tools.

While some children with disabilities may, at times, be able to critically evaluate the affordances of technological features independently, younger learners or those with exceptionalities may need more assistance with this process. Kaczorowski (2015) recently examined children (with and without disabilities) using an interactive mobile technology intervention during the independent portion of math instruction in a grade 4 classroom. Kaczorowski found the children without exceptionalities were readily more able to discover the unique affordances to the technological features incorporated in the intervention (e.g., utilizing different colours to show place value in writing tasks) than children with exceptionalities. This is not to say children with exceptionalities cannot discover things on their own. In this study, children with exceptionalities tended to focus on the intentional AT features like using audio prompts to read word problems aloud as opposed to using the features to support critical thinking and problem-solving tasks. Consequently, inquiry and discovery learning and explicit instruction should not be mutually exclusive practices in classrooms that include children with exceptionalities. Other scholars acknowledge the role of the educator as fluid within an inquiry-based classroom (i.e., co-learners, facilitators, observers, resources, direct instructors; Chiarotto, 2011; Harwood, Bajovic, Woloshyn, Di Cesare, Lane & Scott, 2015; Maloch & Horsey, 2013). Educators should pay attention to individual learners' needs and adapt their role accordingly to provide the supports and scaffolds necessary for each child (e.g., modelling, gradual release of responsibility, corrective and affirmative feedback).

Another consideration when integrating tablets into the inclusive classroom is collaborative learning. Children learn a lot from each other, acting as models and tutors for one another. This learning can occur either informally or in more formal practices. On one occasion during the *Crayons and iPads* study, Jay (a child who had been identified with ASD) grabbed one of the researcher's hands, pointed to the search bar and asked for Veggie Tales. At this point, he was unable to type the request and needed assistance from his peers. A few months later, he was observed engaging in this behaviour independently without peer assistance, and his new abilities were described within the researcher's notes.

Jay was working independently watching previews of Veggie Tales. As he scrolled through the thumbnail list of videos, the researcher asked him about a video he passed featuring a particular character in the show, Larry Boy. Jay scrolled down the screen briefly looking for the video, before deciding to type his request into the search bar. He perfectly spelt 'larry boy' into the search bar, found and selected the video he wanted to watch between the available options.

More formally, highly effective practices for older children such as Peer-Assisted Learning strategies (PALs; What Works Clearinghouse, 2011) can easily be incorporated into activities using mobile technology. Using PALs, children participate in peer tutoring through structured interactions. Educators assign children to pairs based on proficiency; one child is considered proficient in a particular area and the other demonstrates difficulties. Initially, the proficient child begins as the tutor and later becomes the tutee (What Works Clearinghouse, 2011). Educators can implement PALs using tablets to provide peer instruction on the AT tools and features (highlighting, speak selection, word prediction) to familiarize children with their use. Since not every classroom will have access on a one-to-one ratio of tablets to children, thoughtful tablet collaboration among children is beneficial in an inclusive classroom.

CONCLUSION

The thoughtful integration of technology, when combined with research-based effective practices, opens up new possibilities and affordances for learners with exceptionalities. Through our work as teachers and researchers, we have come to view the broadening field of educational technology as inherently fertile grounds for implementing inclusive and empowering approaches to teaching all learners. Inclusive frameworks such as the UDL can help guide how teachers conceptualize and create learning opportunities for children. As illustrated throughout the chapter, emerging mobile technology applications can be used to address a host of barriers experienced by struggling learners and children with exceptionalities. Mobile technology can be incredibly powerful, as it combines elements of assistive and instructional technology, and can engage all learners flexibly and dynamically. Educators must be mindful of how to incorporate mobile technology into their classrooms, while remaining cognizant of the considerations and needs of learners with disabilities. As today's classrooms are comprised of diverse learners with a wide variety of capabilities, including mobile technologies, has important implications for educators in *meeting all children's needs*.

USING iPads TO EMPOWER YOUNG CHILDREN AS READERS AND WRITERS

Vera E. Woloshyn, Arlene Grierson
and Laura Lane

Abstract

In this chapter, we discuss how early childhood educators can use iPads and their associated applications (apps) to support children's reading and writing development, enhance their motivation to engage in these activities, and promote their sense of self-confidence and identity as competent readers and writers. Drawing upon examples from our own research studies and personal experiences, we focus the discussion on how iPads can be used to promote integrated authentic reading and writing experiences, support multisensory learning, strengthen early reading and writing skills, enhance children's access, choice and motivation, and encourage engagement in collaborative reading and writing activities.

Keywords

Reading and Writing, iPads, Multisensory, Collaborative, Motivation and Engagement

INTRODUCTION

Young children's journeys to becoming readers and writers begin in their homes, long before they attend ECE programs (Neumann, Copple & Bredekamp, 2000;

Snow, Burns & Griffin, 1998). In the 21st century, these journeys often include home-based technoliteracy experiences (Marsh, 2004). For instance, after reading the storybook *Goodnight, Goodnight Construction Site* (Duskey Ringer, 2011), Arlene observed her grandson eagerly engage in play with his fleet of toy construction vehicles, pausing as he did so to watch a YouTube video about an excavator on his grandma's iPad. He then resumed imaginary play with his toy vehicles, excitedly singing the song from the video, using the new vocabulary presented within it and relating information from it to that in his book. In this era, such seamless and enthusiastic integration of young children's technoliteracy and traditional play experiences is increasingly commonplace (Common Sense Media, 2013). Indeed, interacting with technology-based systems is an increasingly important aspect of being literate in the 21st century (Burke & Marsh, 2013).

Today, literacy is perceived as complex, multimodal, interconnected processes that enable individuals to use language, symbols, gestures, sounds, images and nonverbal communications in order to develop their knowledge and skills, achieve their goals, communicate effectively with others and participate fully in society. In these ways, being literate involves the ability to generate, understand and communicate information across a variety of contexts (UNESCO, 2006). While we acknowledge the interconnected dimensions of literacy beginning with the foundations of oral language, our primary focus in this chapter is children's reading and writing development.

Young children's reading and writing is most meaningful when it is contextualized within authentic, risk-free activities (Beschorner & Hutchison, 2013; Singh, 2010). Enjoyable play-based authentic learning experiences in early childhood can provoke, ignite and excite young children, thus nurturing these requisite motivations for literacy (Cunningham, 2008). iPads are engaging, motivating tools that have the potential to provide young children with a mosaic of authentic, playful, interest-based, multisensory, multimodal, developmentally appropriate early literacy experiences (Flewitt, Messer & Kucirkova, 2014b; Neumann, 2014; Wong, 2015). As such, iPads are powerful tools that can promote children's reading and writing development across a variety of interconnected dimensions ranging from oral language to visual representation. In this chapter, we illustrate how the integrated and supported use of iPads and their associated applications (apps) can support children's reading and writing development, enhance their motivation to engage in related activities and promote their sense of self-confidence and identity as competent readers and writers (Beschorner & Hutchison, 2013; Flewitt et al., 2014b; Lynch & Redpath, 2014; McPake et al., 2013). Specifically, we draw upon examples from the *Crayons and iPads* study and other literature to discuss how iPads can be used to promote integrated authentic reading and writing experiences, support multisensory learning, strengthen early reading and writing skills, enhance access, choice and motivation, and encourage engagement in collaborative and creative reading and writing activities. While we discuss these benefits separately for clarity, they are interconnected and mutually reinforcing, with each positively affecting the other. For example, the multisensory opportunities provided through using iPads can increase children's motivation, support integrated authentic learning experiences, strengthen early reading and writing skills and encourage collaboration. We conclude that iPads offer early childhood educators a valuable medium for fostering children's early reading and writing.

SUPPORTING INTEGRATED, AUTHENTIC READING AND WRITING EXPERIENCES

iPads are handheld, lightweight and portable, making them ideal technologies for use by young children. Their portability provides children with the option of engaging in a variety of integrated literacy and play-based activities across time, activities and settings (Neumann & Neumann, 2014; O'Mara & Laidlaw, 2011). For instance, Kervin and Mantei (2011) worked with transitioning preschool children to create computer-based digital stories (consisting of digital photos and verbal recordings) that they could use to introduce themselves to their kindergarten teachers. As part of the story-making process, children were charged with staging and photographing themselves (or directing such photos), with many of the children choosing to create narratives using images from their homes or outdoors.

We similarly observed instances of transference from within and outside the classroom in the *Crayons and iPads* study. In one instance, a small group of young children became inspired to create a video about caring for the earth in response to Earth Day activities in their school. Their teacher encouraged the children to take an iPad outside during outdoor play in order to begin to explore ideas about how to care for their playground. In Figure 9.1, two girls discuss the importance of plants and flowers with one of the researchers, explaining that they should not be picked or destroyed. Their ideas were integrated into a more structured video that the children completed subsequently with adult support when they returned indoors. The portability and internal camera of the iPad provided these children with opportunities to extend their classroom learning experiences to their sites of play. Similarly,

Figure 9.1   Children & researcher create an outdoor documentary with iPad

the outdoor play was integrated into their classroom experiences in authentic ways, extending the overall meaningfulness and applicability of their learning experiences. Fluidity and integration across contexts enhances children's learning and reinforces notions of generalization across tasks and environments. In this way, iPads offer children opportunities to engage in reading and writing activities that extend across designated places within and outside of the classroom.

PROMOTING MULTISENSORY LEARNING

When children experience information through multiple modalities including visual, auditory, tactile and/or kinaesthetic representations, their understanding and retention of that information is enhanced (Neumann et al., 2000). Similarly, children's early reading and writing experiences are enhanced when they are encouraged to interact or produce text through multiple modalities. The iPad is a multisensory interactive tool that is easy for young children to operate, providing them with visual, auditory, tactile and kinaesthetic experiences while encouraging creativity, self-expression and curiosity (Beschorner & Hutchison, 2013; Tahnk, 2011).

Reviewing digital texts (e-books) is one example of how iPads can be used to support children's multisensory learning experiences. E-books can provide children with integrated literacy experiences, extending their learning as they listen, view and respond to digital stories (Brueck & Lenhart, 2015). Having children engage with e-books – especially those containing animation, interactive media, hyperlinks that provide definitions and additional information about words and concepts, and dynamic visuals that elaborate and complement main concepts of the text – can enhance comprehension and retention of information as well as provide ongoing motivation for revisiting text (Korat, Levin, Ben-Shabt, Shneor & Bokovza, 2014; Labbo & Kuhn, 2000). Presumably, learning gains experienced through the reading of e-books would extend to reading on iPads.

We observed many children engaged in reading e-books, expressing specific enthusiasm for hotspots (i.e., animated and dynamic visuals and/or text reading software that extend text concepts). In the example below, a young girl excitedly describes a favourite e-book, explaining selected hotspots while demonstrating her story knowledge.

Michelle (pseudonym) opens the Cinderella: Storybook Deluxe App and watches the narrated story alongside her educator [the arrow key at the bottom of the page is used to turn pages]. Michelle clicks the arrow button, moving rapidly across pages. She stops at the page where Cinderella's fairy godmother has arrived and is in search of a carriage to take her to the ball. Michelle turns to her educator and says, 'Watch!' She clicks and the pumpkin is covered in fairy dust and transformed into a carriage. Michelle exclaims, 'Ta Da!' She clicks the next button stating, 'Now watch this' as the mice then turn into horses. She begins to laugh. She continues to click rapidly … waits for a dress to turn into a ball gown and begins eagerly nodding and smiling. She clicks the screen with shoes and as they turn into glass slippers exclaims, 'Slippers! I have slippers.' (Research observations)

Many apps provide similar features as e-books (read-aloud narration, hotspots), as well as additional options that promote creativity and multimodal forms of expression including choices for children to record their retellings (e.g., I Like Books; Disney Princess Story Theatre; Toontastic; Toy Story Read Along), and/or create alternative narratives (e.g., Don't Let the Pigeon Run this App). We observed a number of children engage with various apps to retell and/or reauthor stories, movies, directions and/or documentaries. For instance, a young boy (Bernie) approached Vera wanting to use the Toontastic SHREK app. Vera provided initial support to Bernie by explaining the purpose of the app (i.e., to narrate a movie with a beginning, middle and end, while simultaneously selecting character actions, voices and musical backdrops). They also discussed a possible storyline. When Bernie explained that he 'wants Shrek to get the dragon', Vera helped him to audio-record this statement. With assistance, Bernie proceeded to select character icons (e.g., Shrek, Princess Fiona, donkey), word icons (e.g., brave, mean, funny, happy) and musical interludes for the next scene. After each selection, Bernie and Vera watched the movie progression with Bernie demonstrating increased independence using the function keys. Without prompting he concluded his story with the statement, 'Shrek runs'. He left seemingly satisfied with his creation after viewing the final version. When children engage in retelling and reauthoring activities with iPad apps, they strengthen their understandings of textual information as well as foster connections between listening, speaking, viewing, representing, reading and writing (Beschorner & Hutchison, 2013). Working with children in this multisensory way also prompts them to consider how voice, tone and music can be used to communicate and enhance storytelling, thus increasing their overall understanding about how meaning is conveyed through text (Beschorner & Hutchison, 2013).

STRENGTHENING EARLY READING AND WRITING SKILLS

It is well established that reading with children supports their reading and writing development, with parents, early childhood educators and other adults typically assuming the role of the reader who guides the reading process (Snow et al., 1998). These adults can point to words as they are read out loud, engage children in predictive activities and explore children's responses to text. iPads also can provide children with read-aloud experiences, including text-to-speech tracking functions (e.g., word pointing) and questioning, often with seemingly similar benefits. For instance, having kindergarten children read (and reread) e-books has been demonstrated to enhance their vocabulary, as well as their word reading abilities, with these gains being especially impressive for children whose home environments did not include frequent reading aloud (e.g., Korat, 2010; Korat & Shamir, 2008).

There also is emerging evidence that having children engage with high-quality iPad apps (e.g., Happy Birthday Dog, Grandma's Garden, Grandma's Kitchen, Grandpa's Workshop) can reinforce, strengthen and enhance foundational reading and writing skills. For instance, engaging with tablet-based apps can promote and sustain children's phonological awareness (e.g., recognition of sound units in words), letter recognition, letter–sound correspondence, letter formation and sight word acquisition, with such effects being especially pronounced for children who experience reading challenges and/or those who do not have access to tablets in their homes (Cubelic & Larwin, 2014; Neumann, 2014). We observed many children willingly engage in apps seemingly intended for early literacy development.

> A few children sitting at the table seem to be playing the same game. Lisa is playing Play Square Happy Birthday, Dog! As part of this app, players are required to match letters to corresponding magnets to form words. As she plays, Lisa is stating each letter sound and repeating the word name. She quietly celebrates each success with a soft, 'yah!' Vera asks Lisa to describe the game. Lisa explains that the items are 'hidden' throughout the room. She shows Vera where to find a birthday cake by opening a refrigerator. Lisa retells Vera the story associated with the app (i.e., preparing for the dog's birthday party). She explains that after an item is found, you need to match letters in the room with the word at the bottom of the screen and then draw a box around the word. She explains that sometimes you need to squeeze the letters together and push the word together [blending] and then draw the box around the item. (Research observations)

There are many ways in which engaging with such apps promotes young children's reading and writing development. For instance, most young children find the provision of instant feedback provided through apps as reinforcing (Beschorner & Hutchison, 2013; Flewitt, Kucirkova & Messer, 2014a), especially with repeated use and practice across time (Muis, Ranellucci, Trevors & Duffy, 2015). Furthermore, many children can progress through apps independently and at times and places of their choosing, making them readily useable. In these ways, children may use these apps successfully with and/or without adult input (McManis & Gunnewig, 2012).

ENHANCING ACCESS, CHOICE AND MOTIVATION

Access to and choice over reading materials are two critical elements in enhancing children's motivation to engage in reading (Allington & Gabriel, 2012). iPads are powerful tools that provide unlimited access to a variety of reading materials as available through the Internet, e-books and apps. Providing young children with varied reading materials and choices can help them further develop their understanding of the multiple purposes of communication as well as their genre preferences, inviting repeated reading of preferred texts. Similarly, providing young children with a variety of tools (digital and non-digital) can help shape their understanding of print purposes, functions and formats (Neslihan Bay, 2015). Alongside paper-based writing instruments such as crayons, pencils and markers, we observed many young children using the iPads and associated apps for drawing and story writing. Children appeared especially receptive to options with respect to colour, instruments and illustrations that were incumbent with the iPad. In addition, many children were competent in using the stylus pens that enabled them to navigate the small screens and compact spaces (Couse & Chen, 2010).

Working with iPads and associated apps also can assist children in navigating some of the cognitive and psycholinguistic requirements associated with traditional print materials, including the need to decipher text, form letters and words and use conventional spelling and print. Namely, children are able to use iPad features that assist them to produce conventional text, colourings and other products in an independent fashion (Beschorner & Hutchison, 2013; McManis & Gunnewig, 2012). For instance, children who are yet not capable of producing refined drawings can supplement their iPad creations by selecting well-formed illustrations from among existing photo banks. Alternatively, they can use the camera and video features to capture images and events from their immediate environments (Flewitt et al., 2014a). Children can also use voice dictation and recording functions to represent, explain and/or elaborate their productions, extending their knowledge demonstration and sharing capabilities. Again, the example from our research notes detailed below helps illustrate one of the many instances that we observed of young children using app features to assist them in preparing error-free print materials, thus supporting their writing abilities and enhancing their motivation.

> A couple of children were writing captions for their drawings onto sentence strips. These girls did not like making mistakes. The teacher suggested that they practice writing the words that they didn't know on the iPad (using the Chalk Board app). The children used the styluses to do this writing. They then transferred their words to the sentence strips. (Research notes)

We also observed many children expressing pride in the quality of the products that they produced when working with iPads, viewing their finished productions as polished. For instance, Vera recalls working with Anna while she explored a new colouring app (Hello Crayon). Anna's first efforts appeared tentative and focused on discovering the specific features associated with the app, with Vera gently enquiring about the app functions. Throughout most of the session, Anna erased many of her initial drawings to replace them with ones using more preferable colours and/or textures contained within the app. Indeed much of the drawing session involved drawing an object (e.g., grass,

Figure 9.2 Anna's self-portrait

sun, dirt), erasing the image and redrawing it using a new function (e.g., paint brush, thin line, thick line) (Figure 9.2). Anna appeared to engage in this discovery process with enthusiasm and without frustration, ultimately producing her intended drawing with pride.

In these ways, keyboard and autocorrect functions can often help children create productions that are more sophisticated and closer to conventional text, thus reducing the cognitive demands associated with writing such as alphabet knowledge, print formation and spelling conventions (Flewitt et al., 2014b; Kervin & Mantei, 2011). In addition, iPads can promote children's sense of choice, independence and overall motivation for engaging in reading and writing activities. Through playful exploration, trial-and-error experimentation, sharing and provision of instant feedback, children's motivation for task engagement is enhanced, as is their sense of accomplishment and identities as readers and writers (Flewitt et al., 2014b; Wohlwend, 2010).

FOSTERING COLLABORATION

iPads can help support collaborative reading and writing activities and provide children with multiple, nonlinear entry points into these processes (Flewitt,

Kucirkova & Messer, 2014). For example, children can work together to read a text or create a story, with some children contributing throughout the entire process and others taking on specific roles (e.g., creating a specific illustration, developing a character, providing a story solution). Working with iPads encourages children to engage in collaborative problem-solving while also participating in affirmative and constructive, on-task dialogue (Falloon & Khoo, 2014; Flewitt et al., 2014b).

When children write collaboratively, their motivation is enhanced through a sense of shared purpose and identity as authors (Nolen, 2007). Specifically we observed two young girls, Taylor and Katherine, using the Storybook Maker app to record their thoughts about how to care for the planet. By brainstorming and conversing with each other, the girls engaged in joint planning and negotiated new ideas that extended their text production. They also interacted with their environment by utilizing classroom-based literacy resources (e.g., message of the day, word wall) and enhanced their writing capacities. Together, Taylor and Katherine strengthened their working knowledge of the collaborative process by negotiating their roles and responsibilities as authors and by formulating a plan to audio-record their story.

> Taylor writes the sentence and Katherine draws the picture. Katherine draws herself and her body. The hands are big because she has to fit five fingers on the body. She counts the big fingers to four and then tries to fit a fifth finger on the picture. Taylor tells her it looks like a monster because the hands are so big. There are lots of giggles … They help each other type. Taylor questions 'Where's the I?' Katherine attempts to help her find the letter… After Katherine has finished drawing she asks, 'Can we record our voice?' (Research notes)

Tablets provide children with many formal and/or informal opportunities to share and seek feedback about their productions from their peers, teachers and families (Knobel & Wilber, 2009; Wohlwend, 2010). We witnessed many such sharing experiences, with children eagerly sharing their technological knowledge as related to the iPads and their familiarity of the functions of the device and related apps (e.g., using the internal camera, finding keyboard letters, selecting drawing and photo options). Similarly, the children willingly shared and commented upon one another's productions (i.e., seeking feedback for their development, sharing final products). In the preceding example, Taylor and Katherine assisted each other in locating function keys in favour of taking up Laura's offers of assistance.

Laura reaches over the table to show Taylor and but she pushes Laura's hand away ... the two girls continue to work together. 'I'm looking for black, I mean brown.' Taylor asks Katherine for help. (Research notes)

Given the touch-based nature of the iPad, the device appears to encourage such knowledge sharing, while also providing children with instant, readily understandable feedback (e.g., removal of a spelling error line, screen burst in response to correct response). In these ways, most young children are able to acquire a working knowledge about tablets and their associated functions and apps readily and without frustration (Flewitt et al., 2014b; Lynch & Redpath, 2014).

Providing opportunities for children to share their reading and writing experiences are powerful learning moments as they promote notions of learning expertise among peers and can empower children's willingness to engage in problem-solving activities. We witnessed young children demonstrating pride in presenting their productions (finished or ongoing) to their peers and educators. In many cases, such sharing occurred informally, with children showing and seeking formative feedback from their peers and others as they developed their pictures, plays and stories. In the example below, Lucas experiments with using the Story Maker app, shares his discoveries and develops a story.

Lucas needed assurance to open a new page but then was completely independent. He typed in a title for his story and his name. He immediately found how to use the camera to take pictures and put them in the story. He had fun adding sound. He used both the pre-recorded sounds and he recorded his voice. He was very happy to show one of the research assistants how he put his story together. He also learned to make images bigger and smaller on a page and how to add borders on one of the pages. He independently 'played' his book at various points for his own viewing, to show his friends, to show other researchers and to show his teacher (all at different times). (Research notes)

At other times, knowledge sharing was more formal and involved children presenting their creations and productions to their peers as part of circle or story time. In these ways, using iPads can challenge notions of authoring as an isolated, laborious and single-person process to that of a creative, shared and collaborative one, while nurturing children's sense of accomplishment, pride in their productions and overall engagement in reading and writing processes (Tonn, 2013).

CONCLUDING THOUGHTS

There is little doubt that iPads and other touch-based technologies will continue to have a substantial presence in the lives of young children (Common Sense Media, 2013). Like any other tool however, the iPad is not a panacea and must be used in a balanced and thoughtful manner. The participation of knowledgeable others, including early childhood educators, is especially important for the potential of the iPad to be fully realized (Brueck & Lenhart, 2015; Flewitt et al., 2014b). Educators are encouraged to have children articulate their thinking when interacting with iPads, as engaging in such conversations can provide them with important insights about children's learning processes, critical thinking, problem-solving and creativity that otherwise may not be apparent in viewing their final stories, pictures or other productions (Wohlwend, 2010). To this end, we have provided several examples of children's early reading and writing experiences using iPads as documented within the *Crayons and iPads* study, illustrating synergies between children's imaginary play, exploration and social interactions, as well as educators' promptings, environmental supports and iPad features.

In order to be successful in the 21st century, young children will need to develop critical thinking, communication, collaboration and creativity skills in addition to the traditional skills of reading and writing within and across print and digital mediums (Partnership for 21st Century Learning, 2015). Children's development of these skills and attributes will, in part, be dependent on their interactions with knowledgeable educators and others who can foster supportive learning environments that promote inquiry, exploration and intellectual curiosity. The iPad represents a powerful tool to assist in meeting these objectives and fostering early literacy development, extending the repertoire of resources available to those who work with young children.

10

IT'S AN APP, APP WORLD

Dane Marco Di Cesare

Abstract

From an ECE context, this chapter will focus on reviewing the various forms of tablet apps that can be used to support inquiry-based learning practices. The particular nuances of the varied categories of apps (skill-based, evergreen, sandbox) are reviewed, detailing how their differentiated quality opens a variety of possibilities for inquiry-based learning. With the possibility to shift the child's role from passive participant to (inter)active user, tablet apps can be used to foster meta-cognitive skills and provide opportunities to make meaning in different learning contexts (Wang et al., 2010).

Keywords

Apps, Skill-Based Apps, Evergreen Apps, Sandbox Apps

INTRODUCTION

An inquiry-based pedagogical model requires educators to listen and observe children's attentions, interests and questions, discerning what will *spark* and inspire opportunities for investigation and exploration (Chiarotto, 2011; Harwood, Bajovic, Woloshyn, Di Cesare, Lane & Scott, 2015). As Memme and Winters highlight in this volume, tablet applications (apps) can add a unique layer to the inquiry process, affording children the opportunity to seek and construct knowledge in digital environments through physical manipulation on a touchscreen interface. These interactions are seldom confined to the digital world alone. Movements between physical and digital worlds with naturalized movements and knowledge practices have been noted (Burnett, Merchant, Pahl & Rowsell, 2014). Children negotiate the balance between the physical and digital worlds, using digital landscapes to investigate, explore and interact. Thus, the tablet interface affords a shift of the child's role, moving from passive participant to (inter)active user (Wang et al., 2010). This fluidity of movement not only fosters metacognitive skills but provides opportunities for children to make meaning in different learning contexts (Wang et al., 2010). This chapter will focus on the ways in which apps, when appropriately selected, supported and utilized, can be used to foster an inquiry-based pedagogical approach within ECE classrooms.

APPS FOR EDUCATION

As of June 2016, there were more than two million apps in Apple's App Store (Statista, 2016a), and this number continues to grow. Educational apps represent the third largest app category, following games and business-related apps (Statista, 2016b). Thus, it is no surprise that with the popularity of tablets on the rise, their use in educational settings has seen an increase in recent years (MediaSmarts, 2014). Engagement with quality apps can afford children the opportunity to develop the necessary skills to construct knowledge in an attempt to solve real-world problems and make meaning of the physical world that surrounds them. However, to date, the term 'educational app' has yet to be defined and the industry remains unregulated in terms of assessing if an app is educational or beneficial for learning (Zosh, Hirsh-Pasek, Golinkoff & Parish-Moriss, 2016). Guidelines on assessing the educational value of an app are still emerging (Harwood, 2014; Zosh et al., 2016), and resources are available to help guide educators' choices (e.g., Children's Technology Review[1]; Common Sense Education[2]; Teachers with Apps[3]). This chapter highlights some of research literature exploring the possibilities of apps and ways of thinking about 'educational' apps to ensure selections are based on the goal of fostering an inquiry-based pedagogical approach within ECE classrooms.

Wang et al. (2010) found that technology allows for opportunities for children to engage in critical reflection. For example, children can explore the

---

1   http://childrenstech.com/about

2   www.commonsense.org/education/

3   www.teacherswithapps.com

properties of water with *Max and Ruby Science*, investigate the life cycle and proliferation of plants in a simulated environment using *Plants*, and investigate the function and use of a variety of simple machines in *Simple Machines*. Further, views or experimental conditions can be created using technology that could not exist otherwise (Wang et al., 2010). For example, children can explore environmental changes over time using NASA's Images of Change Earth Images app, instantly explore a variety of different cultural houses around the world using *Homes*, or explore the human body systems in *The Human Body*. In addition, with quick access to the Internet, communication apps like *FaceTime*, *Skype* or *Google Hangout* can connect classrooms around the world. The mobility of the tablet invites portability and use throughout the classroom, from the traditional 'circle' rug to centres, desks or even outside activities. While the tablet can be used in a myriad of ways, most commonly educators utilize skill-based apps (Daccord, 2013; Di Cesare & Kaczorowski, 2014).

SKILL-BASED APPS

Many educational apps can be considered skill-based, that is, they focus on fostering the development of a discrete skill or concept. A skill-based app may focus on building automaticity with simple math facts, identifying letter sounds and patterns or identifying colours. For example, *Kindergarten Math: Drills in Addition, Subtraction, Comparison* is used to determine the accuracy and speed with which children can solve ten addition, subtraction and/or comparison problems.

The quality of skill-based apps plays a large role in enhancing learning experiences in the classroom. Without specific direction, it may be difficult for educators to determine the quality of specific apps. Individual learners use many skill apps independently, and as such they should be used to target individualized needs. Thus, the apps selected should be those that are reflective of situated practices, engaging, provide immediate feedback and allow for learner growth. Apps chosen should also consider the potential ceiling effect for a learner. This ceiling effect occurs when the app becomes too easy and the child is no longer challenged. Walker (2011) supports this notion of evaluating skill-based apps and further promotes the use of a rubric to evaluate their effectiveness based on six categories: curriculum connection, authenticity, feedback, differentiation, user-friendliness and student motivation. In terms of curriculum connection, apps should relate to the curriculum, aligning with target skills and/or concepts (Walker, 2011). It should be noted that several of these characteristics (authenticity, user-friendliness, student motivation) could be used to evaluate other types of apps, such as Evergreen and Sandbox apps, which will be discussed later in the chapter.

Another characteristic of an effective app (skill-based, evergreen, sandbox) is the level of authenticity, or the extent to which learners can experience genuine learning experiences. Very few skill-based apps utilize authentic experiences; most tend to be either decontextualized or of the drill-and-skill variety. Conversely, sandbox apps, which will be discussed in greater detail later in the chapter, tend to include authentic learning experiences. When children engage in authentic learning experiences, they tend to be more focused and invested in the experience (Ableser, 2005). Apps that foster authentic learning experiences afford opportunities for learners to take an active role within a real-world context. Thus, children can navigate the digital environment experiencing successes and failures, trying to learn which approaches yield success and those that result in failures (Galarneau, 2005; Price & Rogers, 2004). For example, apps that mimic real-life shopping experiences to develop money-related skills are more effective than decontextualized apps that merely require children to select specific coins or bills.

Constructive and timely feedback is another marker of quality; such feedback can include hints to direct children to the correct answers, branching responses or attending to answers that are partially correct. Apps with immediate feedback have shown to be beneficial for children in learning tasks (Kaczorowski, 2015; Kucirkova, Messer, Sheehy & Panadero; 2014; McClanahan, Williams, Kennedy & Tate, 2012). Immediate feedback can also aid learners in finding the correct answer before mistakes are internalized. Further, as students use many skill apps independently, a feature that summarizes the data on child performance is incredibly useful; this way the educator can evaluate student performance without having to directly observe the child utilizing the app.

The ability to set difficulty levels and control settings to individualize instruction is vital in quality skill-based apps (Hung, Sun & Yu, 2015; Walker, 2011). If an app has only one difficulty setting or level of challenge, it is impossible to meet the needs of the diverse learners within a typical classroom. In addition, limited levels of challenge have implications for motivation and continued use of the app. Hung, Sun & Yu (2015) found that children preferred the challenge mode of *Motion Math: Hungry Fish* (difficulty increased after level completion) over the matching mode setting (set difficulty levels that did not increase). In addition, built-in accessibility features, such as highlighting text or reading text aloud, are also vital in apps. Reading text aloud is an important feature in ECE settings, as children may not have developed the reading skills necessary to read on-screen text. If an app does not have built-in reading fea-tures or selectable text, it is difficult for struggling or non-readers to access the app content independently.

Another factor that contributes to the quality and utility of an app is the level of user-friendliness or ease of use. This refers to the intuitive nature of the app and the ease with which children can effectively use an app without a lot of adult instruction (Walker, 2011). Like other forms of technology, devices or programs that are difficult to use are often abandoned (Henderson & Yeow, 2012; Phillips & Zhao, 1993). Non-intuitive apps require much more instruc-tion and support, requiring time that is often in short supply in a busy ECE classroom. Intuitive apps are also less frustrating for young learners. When an app becomes frustrating, it can lead to avoidance of the app, abandonment during play or resistance when prompted to use the app.

Child motivation is another factor educators should consider when evalu-ating the quality of apps. Motivation is necessary for involvement in learning activities and contributes to the effectiveness of learning (Malone & Lepper, 1987). In addition, motivation can also impact the amount of attention paid to educational apps (Vogel, Kennedy & Kwok, 2009). Motivational features of an app can be determined by examining the novelty, quality and quantity of successful child experiences, level of challenge and overall quality of the app (Hung et al., 2015; Walker, 2011). Even with direct app–curriculum links, authentic learning experiences, immediate feedback and ease of use, if an app does not appeal to children it may not be successfully used.

Assessing the appeal of apps can be challenging; thus, observing children utilizing tablets can benefit an educator in determining which specific apps are motivating for a particular group of learners (Walker, 2011).

While the utilization of skill-based apps in a classroom to target specific skill building has merit, I argue that the full capabilities of tablets are better achieved by the use of evergreen apps. The term evergreen app has been used by edu-cational technology specialists such as Tom Daccord, Tanya Avrith and Frasier Spiers to refer to apps that afford children a wide range of uses. Evergreen apps tend to be focused on creativity and provide children multiple opportunities to explain their thinking or demonstrate their understanding (Avrith, 2014).

EVERGREEN APPS

Evergreen apps are much more flexible than skill-based apps and allow for greater customization. In addition, evergreen apps can be used for cross-curricular activities, and they are not bound by instruction of a particular skill or concept (Daccord, 2013). Evergreen apps are extremely versatile, and they can be used to consume, curate, collaborate and create, often fostering higher-order thinking skills in the process. Educational technology consultants, such as Tom Daccord, call for higher and more effective use of tablets in the classroom, following a 'one screen' model (all apps fit on one screen) and being composed exclusively of evergreen apps (Daccord, 2013).

Many educators attempt to find apps that align perfectly with concepts or ideas they wish to teach (e.g., teaching about the seasons and using an app related to seasons). Though the Apple Store is filled with hundreds of thousands of apps, such specificity is not always available or appropriate. Complicating matters, educators are often faced with procedural barriers (e.g., school-based policies, inability to make paid app purchases) that limit their ability to download new apps (Di Cesare & Kaczorowski, 2014). In light of this, the functionality, utility and versatility of evergreen apps are beneficial. Evergreen apps are not bound to specific content or ideas, so they can be used to align with any curricular activity. Furthermore, as evergreen apps can be utilized continually for a variety of different tasks, children can become familiar with their use, eliminating the learning curve with each new activity. Returning to the example of seasons, an evergreen app like *Shadow Puppet Edu* would enable the child to record, narrate and annotate images of different seasons. There are many different evergreen apps educators may find useful (Di Cesare, 2014), including drawings apps, multimodal authoring apps, collaborative whiteboard apps, digital notebook and annotation apps, or screen recording apps. With these types of apps, countless activities are provided that foster child production, creation and/or collaboration.

Examples of Evergreen Apps

Drawing apps are versatile and effective, provided they allow users to draw freely, allow access to a variety of tools (e.g., crayons, pencils, markers, acrylic brushes, watercolour brushes) and features (e.g., layers, insertion of photos, export ability). Effective drawing apps contain a variety of tools and offer children opportunities to freely create without feeling restricted to a particular art style. More advanced drawing apps mimic the authentic look and feel of their physical counterparts, giving more digital realism to crayon and brush strokes. The ability to insert layers and photos within a drawing app is vital in its classification as a quality evergreen app. This allows children to create artwork in layers, perhaps drawing the outline of a drawing on one layer and filling it in on a lower layer. The ability to import photos or images is important as it allows children to annotate and/or blend media styles. In addition, the ability to export the created content is also vital; this feature allows the creation to be used in conjunction with other apps. Some examples of evergreen drawing apps with these quality features include *Paper* by 53, *Tayasui Sketches+* and *Sketchbook Pro*.

Multimodal authoring apps permit children to combine image (still or video), sound and/or text to create complex, multifaceted compositions. The benefits of multimodal authoring apps are well established as these apps allow learners to create high-quality artefacts with multiple layers of meaning (Di Cesare, 2015; Vasudevan, Schultz & Bateman, 2010). In addition, multimodal authoring apps can be used in conjunction with drawing apps. Multimodal authoring apps can either be video-based (e.g., *iMovie, Toontastic, Puppet Pals, Puppet Pals II*) or book-based (e.g., *My Story Book Creator*). Video-based multimodal authoring apps result in video outputs, with the format dictated by the type of tablet. Artefacts created in book-based multimodal authoring apps can be exported in a variety of formats, including movie files, web-based, e-book, iBook, or PDF. When selecting a quality book-based multimodal authoring app, it is important to consider the availability of exporting options. For example, it is more useful to publish books to a web version, preserving multimodal features such as narration and video (versus publishing as a PDF which removes narration and video). When children create digital books, digital video compositions or other works, sharing those works across contexts is important (class, school, community, globe); thus, publishing capability is a key consideration.

Screen recording apps are one of the most powerful evergreen apps in that they allow children to capture their thinking or showcase their understanding (e.g., *Explain Everything* and *Shadow Puppet Edu*). These apps invite users to import images (still or video), PDF or presentation documents, or other types of files. Inherent with these apps is the ability to annotate these files and record audio. This flexibility offers limitless uses, as children are able to record their thinking or processes as they work within the app. Some of these apps allow learners to create new content, in addition to annotating content that was authored using another app. Effective screen recording apps have exporting options, allowing finished pieces of the child's work to be moved from the tablet to a cloud or another storage option. This is important as the device storage capacity of a tablet is quite limited, and video files created with screen casting apps do require a lot of space.

SANDBOX APPS

Sandbox apps refer to apps that are open-ended without specified directions and goals. Thus, the child's interaction and experience with the app can change each time. The *Toca Boca* collection (i.e., *Toca Kitchen 2*, *Toca Life: City*, *Toca Band*, *Toca Train*) and *Tinybop* series (i.e., *The Human Body*, *Plants*, *Homes*, *The Robot Factory*) are vivid examples of sandbox apps. Sandbox apps typically mimic authentic experiences and engage children in diverse digital worlds.

Toca Kitchen 2 is a sandbox app centred on the authentic experience of cooking and preparing food for others. In the app, children can select food items from a fridge and cook and/or prepare the items in a variety of ways (e.g., boil, chop, deep fry, pan fry, salt, add lemon). When food is cooked within the app, it takes on the authentic characteristics based on the selected cooking method. For example, pan-frying too long in the app can yield a charred piece of fish, and deep-frying delivers crispy potato fries (or crisps). Further adding to the authenticity of the experience, this app allows the user to pretend to feed the prepared food to a variety of characters. Each character has a series of likes and dislikes and will respond appropriately based on the type of food offered. For example, one of the depicted characters displays enjoyment with eating boiled carrots (e.g., happy smile), but if the child selects to add too much salt, the character then displays displeasure (e.g., protruding tongue).

Another sandbox app, *Robot Factory* by Tinybop, invites children to construct robots using a variety of tools and parts. After robots are created, the user can test the robot to see if it can walk, run and/or fly in real-world situations. These simulations have various built-in virtual dangers that the robots must either avoid or overcome (e.g., bees, fire, pitfalls) and children must decide how to navigate these obstacles. Another app in the Tinybop series, *The Human Body*, which permits the child to record questions by pressing and holding the screen. These audio recordings are sent to the 'parent' account and can be answered or addressed by a parent or educator. Consequently, sandbox apps, such as those from the Toca Boca and Tinybop series, can provide unique, engaging and open-ended play experiences that work well within an inquiry-based ECE classroom.

CONCLUDING THOUGHTS

While tablets can be extremely motivating for young children to use (Ciampa & Gallagher, 2013), there are important considerations when using and selecting apps with the goal of provoking interests and constructing knowledge within an inquiry-based classroom. First, the manner in which tablets are first introduced to children is significant. When the devices are introduced as *tools for inquiry*, promoted as devices for research and construction of knowledge, the children will adopt tablets in ways that support and complement the answering of their queries. Alternatively, when tablets are introduced as a reward or a simple distraction device, children tend to avoid the richer knowledge construction potential of many apps. Moreover, when used as a reward and a loss of access occurs, the child misses out on valuable learning experiences (Kaczorowski & Di Cesare, 2014). In addition, considering many children may be exposed to devices at home, it is important to contemplate the distinction between the functionality and purpose of tablets in school (e.g., to support learning) and out-of-school environments (e.g., entertainment and learning).

In the ECE classroom, tablets can be a useful resource to support inquiry-based learning practices. Careful consideration is needed when educators select apps for use in their classrooms, namely educators need to be mindful of the type and quality of apps that will be utilized. Skill-based apps should be critically evaluated before situated within teaching practices. These types of apps are frequently employed, often with little critical evaluation beforehand. As such, many of these apps do not directly meet children's specific and individualized needs. Therefore, educators must be thoughtful and intentional with app selections; other types of apps, such as evergreen or sandbox apps, should be downloaded in addition to high-quality skill-based apps. Moreover, educators should consider making greater use of evergreen apps in the classroom. These apps provide children with multimodal avenues for expressing their ideas and thoughts. In an ECE context, multimodal avenues are critical as children have typically not developed advanced writing skills, and utilization of audio, motion and video can provide insight into their thinking. In addition, sandbox apps allow children to play and interact in authentic digital worlds. These apps can be used to create role-play experiences that are rich, variable, contextually relevant and respectful of the 21st-century child's way of being in the world. Ultimately, when carefully selected and used appropriately, tablets (and apps) afford children more agency in their learning, providing a means to construct knowledge and make meaning.

11

LINGERING THOUGHTS

Debra Harwood

Throughout this book, I as the editor – and the contributing authors – have situated technologies, specifically iPads, as a valuable medium for learning. Each chapter has offered snapshots from select studies to help highlight the ways in which the 21st-century child actively and purposefully draws upon a range of everyday experiences to make sense of their world – learning experiences that increasingly include the digital world. Currently, there is a dearth of research focusing on the ways in which technologies influence learning, and many questions remain unanswered. However, as Stephen and Plowman highlight, 'digital technologies and playthings are just one part of the complex and contingent sociocultural environment in which children live and learn' (2014, p. 339). As evidence of this complexity, multiple instances where children's digital/non-digital worlds collided, converged and blurred were highlighted throughout the book. Young children are capable and dynamic consumers, producers and inventors of knowledge (Rowsell & Harwood, 2015). They appear to draw equally upon the visual, gestural, audio and linguistic modes within their play and learning endeavours. The affordances inherent with an iPad (and other mobile technologies) invite multiple meaning-making avenues, assets that must be leveraged within the conceptualization and enactment of curricula and pedagogies for young learners.

Using Dyson's (2013, p. 406) notion of 'children as located somebodies', this book has offered insight into the ways in which children draw upon everyday experiences, thoughts, interactions, cultures and contexts to make meaning of their world – experiences that are *both* digital and non-digital. Learning is messy, multidimensional, fluid, holistic and rooted within sociocultural interactions and local spaces (Dyson, 2013). Children's lives seep into the classroom as regularly as the classroom trickles into families' homes. And digital modes should not be privileged within any context. Rather, children appear to quite naturally rely on a web of images, sounds, moving images, materials, conversations and interactions and so on to think, play and narrate their understandings of the world. This idea of the web or nexus can help foster rethinking of traditional binaries within education while also providing insight into ways of fostering and encouraging invitational learning spaces.

RETHINKING BINARIES WITHIN EDUCATION

Orientations that position technology alongside other modes for children's explorations, creations, musings and learning can help disrupt the binaries that often plague education (e.g., child-centred teacher-directed, nature–culture binaries, etc.). The Loris Malaguzzi International Centre in Reggio Emilia, Italy, recently displayed an exhibit entitled *Bordercrossings*. The exhibit focused on the 'digital poetic', specifically documenting the plurality and amalgam of multiple modes of communication and representation of children's thinking. As the exhibit aptly depicted:

> Technology enters the everyday, not dominating, not replacing, but mixing with other languages. It enters as an environment, not strictly instrumental and functional, but rather as the connector of multidisciplinary learning and explorations, supporting children's ways of knowing, inaugurating new environments of socialisation and sharing, in which each child's 'mental world' finds a possible representation. (Loris Malaguzzi International Centre, 2016)

Children appear to move fluidly between the multitudes of learning spaces available to them and are less fixated on delineating between constructs such as play and learning, formal-informal, digital and non-digital. For a child, cooking within the *Grandma's Kitchen* app is 'real' and typically twinned with dramatic play in the kitchen area of the classroom. In our studies cited throughout the book, the convergence of this concrete and digital worlds created 'hybrid/intertextual' spaces for learning (Di Cesare, Harwood & Rowsell, 2016). From the child's perspective, learning and play are inseparable and, as Rose and her colleagues explain in this volume, digital playfulness can co-exist alongside other play pursuits within a thoughtful and intentionally constructed learning space.

SETTING A LEARNING CONTEXT FOR DIGITAL PLAY

Karen Wohlwend's (2011) conceptualization of play as a tactic has helped frame much of the thinking in this book. And throughout, we have illustrated the digital playfulness of an iPad and the potential contribution the device offers in creating an invitational space, a nexus for children's play and learning to unfold.

> The digital has the potential to transform teaching-learning contexts, offering children's thoughts and theories new modes of representation, proposing a dimension of culture, capable of merging the abstract with the artisanal. Children simultaneously act on plural levels of representation in these digital contexts, exercising a form of hybrid, integrated flexible thinking. (Loris Malaguzzi International Centre, 2016)

Albeit illustrations of this nexus were drawn from research-supported classrooms and a university lab school – and like others who have expressed similar concerns (Vasquez & Felderman, 2013) – we too question whether curricula within ECE supports an orientation of digital playfulness. Purposefully, throughout this volume, my fellow authors and I have privileged children's questions and inquiry pursuits – for us a natural milieu for merging play, learning and iPads. Deleuze and Guattari (1987) wrote, 'children's questions are poorly understood if they are not seen as question-machines' (p. 256). Honouring children's questions and modes of representation seems to be *one* way of supporting children's agency in the classroom while also authenticating their digital knowledge and experiences (Harwood et al., 2015). Supporting these types of classroom communities of inquiry requires an educator who is curious, flexible and collaborative with an orientation to teaching/learning as a shared responsibility among all protagonists, including children.

WHAT THE CHILDREN TAUGHT US

Angry Birds and *Ninja* apps are not allowed at school; there is no such thing as girl and boy apps; a stylus is a real pen; easy apps are boring; and as children, we can negotiate, critique and teach each other. Of course, this simple list represents a mere snippet of the many insights we have garnered in our encounters with children and iPads. The coherent thread throughout this learning and writing journey was the idea that *listening* is a central 'premise for any learning relationship' (Rinaldi, 2006, p. 65), and listening requires a sensitivity and openness to the interconnections between people, materials and discourses (Lenz Taguchi, 2010). The iPad is a material object that relates to the body, imaginations and emotions of children, connecting children to others, to ideas and experiences, and varied places and spaces. The crayon *and* iPad are synonymous tools for learning, and making space for both within ECE can lead to new and unexpected discoveries. As we have learned from children, the iPad can propose alternate forms of play possibilities – converged spaces for learning and experiencing the world where there is little need for binary thinking. Amy, one of the research participants I had met, reminds me of the importance of honouring children's knowledge, affinity for learning and communicating in multiple modes, and the power of imagination when she created a photo story without words.

> Amy is using the iPad and taking pictures of a documentation panel displaying photos of a visit to the classroom from the children's grandparents. She tells me that she wasn't there on the day the photos were taken. I ask her if she'd like to add words to her story. She says no, and proceeds to tell the researcher a photo story from her imagination. She says, 'You can make any story'. Amy affirms that she doesn't really know what happened that day so a made-up story with just pictures is better. (Research observations)

CRAYONS AND iPads

Our journey alongside children's play and explorations with iPads has provided many insights into their interests, competencies and modes of seeing and being in this digital world they inhabit. Children's digital habitus is distinct, uniquely contributing to the ways in which they are forging habits with materials (both digital and non-digital) as they seamlessly move across and within the various modes of representation made available to them. Clearly, the challenge of ensuring access and equity is foundational, as well as nurturing supportive pedagogies for these 21st-century children 'who participate in the world with new mindsets, identities, and practices that impact their lives at home, at school, and beyond' (Vasquez & Felderman, 2013, pp. 2–3).

Invitational learning contexts are key. An invitational space invites and supports children's queries, values the unlimited potential of each child, and fosters curiosity, wonderment and creativity. The child's way of being in this world must be valued. An invitational learning classroom is one where the educator is flexible, able to think laterally and comfortable operating in-between spaces (Kendrick, 2005). Efficacious educators will find ways of promoting the intersections between iPads and children inquiries, while also acknowledging and appreciating the complexity of the critical social negotiations and positioning of power that occurs when iPads are included in the classroom.

New technologies, like the iPad, offer new ways of thinking about the nature of play and learning in ECE. As technologies continue to impact children's lives, blurring the boundaries between online and offline, material and immaterial, local and global contexts, much more research will be needed. Understanding the ways in which the fluidity of the digital world, the converged spaces and the continuum of online and offline contexts the child inhabits impact learning and teaching is foundational. Clearly, in the future, play will persist as a 'continuous process of appropriation, accommodation, assimilation and/or adaption … no matter how far developments in technology change the range of media available to children' (Marsh & Bishop, 2014, p. 77). The digital native is present in our classrooms. Consequently, the responsibility resides with researchers and educators to ensure curricula and pedagogies *provoke, ignite* and *excite* children's curiosities and explorations of the world around them. Crayons *and* iPads coexisting, co-mingling and converging within play and learning contexts seems like an obvious place to start.

REFERENCES

Ableser, J. (2005). Mismatched curriculum: One size does not fit all. *Curriculum and Teaching, 20*(2), 23–40.

Ahrentzen, S., & Evans, G. W. (1984). Distraction, privacy, and classroom design. *Environment and Behavior, 16*(4), 437–454.

Allington, R., & Gabriel, R. (2012). Every child, every day. *Educational Leadership, 69*(6), 10–15.

Amiel, T. (2006). Mistaking computers for technology: Technology literacy and the digital divide. *AACE Journal, 14*(3), 235–256.

Anderson, K. (2009). Applying position theory to the analysis of classroom interactions: Mediating micro-identities, macro kinds, and ideologies of knowing. *Linguistics and Education, 209*, 291–310.

Archer, A. L., & Hughes, C. A. (2010). *Explicit instruction: Effective and efficient teaching.* New York, NY: Guilford Press.

Armenta, A., Serrano, A., Cabrera, M., & Conte, R. (2012). The new digital divide: The confluence of broadband penetration, sustainable development, technology adoption and community participation. *Information Technology for Development, 18*(4), 345–353. doi:10.1080/02681102.2011.625925.

Armstrong, A., & Casement, C. (2000). *The child and the machine: How computers put our children's education at risk.* Beltsville, MD: Robins Lane Press.

Assistive Technology Act, 29 U.S.C. § 3001 et seq. (2004).

Atkinson, K. (2014). Beyond red week: Working with inquiry in early years settings. *Canadian Children, 39*(3), 53–57.

Attewell, P. (2001). The first and second digital divides. *Sociology of Education, 74*(3), 252–259.

Avrith, T. (2014, May). *Digital student portfolios: Redefining assessment using GAFE and iPads.* Lecture presented at CONNECT Conference in Niagara Falls, ON.

Baker, J. M., & Zigmond, N. (1990). Are regular education classes equipped to accommodate students with learning disabilities? *Exceptional children, 56*(6), 515–526.

Barad, K. (2007). *Meeting the universe halfway: Quantum physics and the entanglement of matter and meaning.* Durham, NC: Duke University Press.

Barell, J. (2010). Problem-based learning: The foundation for 21st century skills. In J. Bellanca & R. Brandt (Eds.), *21st century skills: Rethinking how students learn* (pp. 175–200). Bloomington, IN: Solution Tree Press.

Beishuizen, J. (2011). Fostering self-regulated learning in technology enhanced learning environments: Evidence from empirical research. In R. Carneiro, P. Lefrere, K. Steffens, & J. Underwood (Eds.), *Self-regulated learning in technology enhanced environments: A European perspective* (Vol. 5). Rotterdam, The Netherlands: Sense Publishers.

Beschorner, B., & Hutchison, A. (2013). iPads as a literacy teaching tool in early childhood. *International Journal of Education in Mathematics, Science, and Technology, 1*(1), 16–24.

Bishop, J., & Curtis, M. (Eds.). (2001). *Play today in the primary school playground: Life, learning, and creativity.* Buckingham, UK: Open University Press.

Black, R. W. (2010). The language of Webkinz: Early childhood literacy in an online virtual world. *Digital Culture & Education (DCE), 2*(1), 7–24.

Blackwell, C. K., Wartella, E., Lauricella, A. R., & Robb, A. M. (2015). *Technology in the lives of educators and early childhood programs: Trends in access, use, and professional development 2012–2014.* Evanston, Illinois: Center on Media and Human Development at Northwestern University.

Bodrova, E., & Leong, D. (2010). Revisiting Vygotskian perspectives on play and pedagogy. In S. Rogers (Ed.), *Rethinking play and pedagogy in early childhood education: Concepts, contexts, and cultures* (pp. 60–73). New York, NY: Taylor & Francis.

Bourdieu, P. (1977). *Outline of a theory of practice.* Cambridge, UK: Cambridge University Press.

Bourdieu, P. (1986). The forms of capital. In J. Richardson (Eds.), *Handbook of theory and research for the sociology of education* (pp. 46–58). New York, NY: Greenwood.

Bruce, B. C., & Bishop, A. P. (2002). Using the Web to support inquiry-based literacy development. *Journal of Adolescent & Adult Literacy, 45*(8), 706–714.

Bruce, B. C., & Casey, L. (2012). The practice of inquiry: A pedagogical 'sweet spot' for digital literacy? *Computers in the Schools, 29*(1/2), 191–206. doi:10.1080/073 80569.2012.657994.

Brueck, J. S., & Lenhart, L. A. (2015). E-books and TPACK: What teachers need to know. *The Reading Teacher, 68*(5), 373–376. doi:10.1111/1469-7610.ep11903728.

Bruner, J. (1977). *The process of education.* Cambridge, MA: Harvard University Press.

Buchholz, B., Shively, K., Peppler, K., & Wohlwend, K. (2014). Hands on, hands off: Gendered access in crafting and electronics practices. *Mind, Culture, and Activity, 21*(4), 278–297.

Burke, A. M., & Marsh, J. (2013). *Children's virtual play worlds: Culture, learning, and participation.* New York, NY: Peter Lang.

Burnett, C. (2015). (Im)materialising literacies. In J. Rowsell & K. Pahl (Eds.), *The Routledge handbook of literacy studies* (pp. 520–531). London, UK: Routledge.

Burnett, C., Merchant, G., Pahl, K., & Rowsell, J. (2014). The (Im)materiality of literacy: The significance of subjectivity to new literacies research. *Discourse: Studies in the Cultural Politics of Education, 35*(1), 90–103.

Carr, M. (2001). *Assessment in early childhood settings: Learning stories.* London, UK: Sage.

Carr, M., & Lee, W. (2012). *Learning stories: Constructing learner identities in early education.* London, UK: Sage.

Carrington, V. (2013). An argument for assemblage theory: Integrated spaces, mobility, policentricity. In A. Burke & J. Marsh (Eds.), *Children's virtual play worlds: Culture, learning and participation* (pp. 200–216). New York, NY: Peter Lang.

Carter, M. (2007). Making your environment 'the third teacher'. *Exchange, 176*, 22–26.

Castells, M. (2000). *The rise of the network society.* Oxford, UK: Blackwell.

Cavanaugh, B. (2013). Performance feedback and teachers' use of praise and opportunities to respond: A review of the literature. *Education & Treatment of Children, 36*(1), 111–137.

Chai, Z., Vail, C. O., & Ayres, K. M. (2015). Using an iPad application to promote early literacy development in young children with disabilities. *The Journal of Special Education, 48*(4), 268–278.

Chen, B., Gallagher-Mackay, K., & Kidder, A. (2014). Digital learning in Ontario schools: The 'new normal.' *People for Education.* Retrieved from www.peoplefor education.ca/wp-content/uploads/2014/03/digital-learning-2014-WEB.pdf

Chiarotto, L. (2011). *Natural curiosity: Building children's understanding of the world through environmental inquiry: A resource for teachers.* Toronto, ON: Ontario Institute for Studies in Education: University of Toronto Press.

Chung, L., & do Prado Leite, J. C. S. (2009). On non-functional requirements in software engineering. In A. I. Borgida, V. Chaudhri, P. Giorgini, & E. Yu (Eds.), *Conceptual modeling: Foundations and applications* (pp. 363–379). Berlin, Germany: Springer.

Ciampa, K., & Gallagher, T. L. (2013). Getting in touch: Use of mobile devices in the elementary classroom. *Computers in the Schools, 30*(4), 309–328. doi:10.1080/0 7380569.2013.846716.

Clements, D. H., & Sarama, J. (2003). Strip mining for gold: Research and policy in educational technology – A response to 'fool's gold'. *AACE Journal, 11*(1), 7–69.

Cobb-Moore, C., Danby, S., & Farrell, A. (2009). Young children as rule-makers. *Journal of Pragmatics, 44*, 1477–1492.

Colbert, J. (2012). *Welcome to a world of possibilities: Exploring digital technology in early childhood education.* Retrieved from www.elp.co.nz/files/colbert_j_welcome_to_a_world_of_possibilities.pdf

Common Sense Media. (2013). *Zero to eight: Children's media use in America 2013.* Retrieved from www.commonsensemedia.org/research/zero-to-eight-childrens-media-use-in-america-2013#

Compaine, B. (2001). *The digital divide: Facing a crisis or creating a myth?* Cambridge, MA: MIT Press.

Copple, C., Bredekamp, S., & National Association for the Education of Young Children. (Eds.). (2009). *Developmentally appropriate practice in early childhood programs serving children from birth through age 8* (3rd ed.). Washington, DC: National Association for the Education of Young Children.

Cordes, C., & Miller, E. (Eds.). (2000). *Fool's gold: A critical look at computers in childhood.* College Park, MD: Alliance for Childhood.

Corsaro, W. A. (2011). *The sociology of childhood.* Thousand Oaks, CA: Pine Forge Press.

Coughlan, S. (2014, December 3). *Tablet computers in 70% of schools.* Retrieved from www.bbc.com/news/education-30216408.

Couse, L. J., & Chen, D. W. (2010). A tablet for young children? Exploring its viability for early childhood education. *Early Childhood Education, 43*(1), 75–98. doi:10.10 80/15391523.2010.10782562.

Craft, A. (2000). *Creativity across the primary curriculum: Framing and developing practice.* New York, NY: Routledge.

Cromdal, J. (2001). Can I be with? Negotiating play entry in a bilingual school. *Journal of Pragmatics, 33,* 515–543.

Cuban, L. (2009). *Oversold and underused: Computers in the classroom.* Cambridge, MA: Harvard University Press.

Cubelic, C. C., & Larwin, K. H. (2014). The use of iPad technology in the kindergarten classroom: A quasi-experimental investigation of the impact on early literacy skills. *Comprehensive Journal of Educational Research, 2*(4), 47–59.

Cullen, J., Richards, S. B., & Frank, C. L. (2009). Using software to enhance the writing skills of students with special needs. *Journal of Special Education Technology, 23*(2), 33–43.

Cunningham, D. D. (2008). Literacy environment quality in preschool and children's attitudes toward reading and writing. *Literacy Teaching and Learning, 12*(2), 19–36.

Cviko, A., McKenney, S., & Voogt, J. (2014). Teacher roles in designing technology-rich learning activities for early literacy: A cross-case analysis. *Computers & Education, 72,* 68–79. doi:10.1016/j.compedu.2013.10.014.

Daccord, T. (2013, May 28). *The 'evergreen' iPad: Why all your apps should fit on one screen.* Retrieved from www.eschoolnews.com/2013/05/28/the-evergreen-ipad-why-all-your-apps-should-fit-on-one-screen/

Dahlberg, G., & Lenz Taguchi, H. (1994). *Preschool and school: Two different traditions and the vision of a meeting-place.* Stockholm, SE: HLS Förlag.

Davies, B., & Harré, R. (1990). Positioning: The discursive production of selves. *Journal for the Theory of Social Behaviour, 20*(1), 43–63.

Davies, B., & Hunt, R. (1994). Classroom competencies and marginal positionings. *British Journal of Sociology of Education, 15,* 389–408.

Dede, C. (2010). Comparing frameworks for 21st century skills. In J. Bellanca & R. Brandt (Eds.), *21st century skills: Rethinking how students learn* (pp. 51–76). Bloomington, IN: Solution Tree Press.

Deleuze, G., & Guattari, F. (1987). *A thousand plateaus: Capitalism and schizophrenia.* Minneapolis, MN: University of Minneapolis Press.

Di Cesare, D. M. (2014, November). *Apps for inquiry: Using mobile technology to support inquiry based practices.* Lecture presented at CEC TED in Indianapolis, IN.

Di Cesare, D. M. (2015). *'This really shows what I'm trying to say': Exploring how students with disabilities compose with digital video and print* (Doctoral dissertation). University at Buffalo, Buffalo, NY.

Di Cesare, D. M., Harwood, D., Julien, K., & Scott, K. (2015). *There's an app for that? Examining and fostering early childhood educator's content knowledge & use of iPads within early learning contexts.* Unpublished raw data.

Di Cesare, D., Harwood, D., & Rowsell, J. (2016). It is real colouring? Mapping children's im/material thinking in a digital world. In L. Mellinee & B. Guzzetti (Eds.), *Handbook of research on the societal impact of digital media* (pp. 69–93). New York, NY: IGI Global.

Di Cesare, D. M., & Kaczorowski, T. (2014, October). *Bypassing barriers and securing solutions: A paradigm shift in mobile technology implementation.* Lecture presented at NYS CEC Conference in Syracuse, NY.

Dietze, B., & Kashin, D. (2011). *Playing and learning in early childhood education.* Toronto, ON: Pearson.

Duskey Ringer, S. (2011). *Goodnight, goodnight construction site*. San Francisco, CA: Chronicle Books.

Dyson, A. H. (1997). *Writing superheroes: Contemporary childhood, popular culture, and classroom literacy*. New York, NY: Teachers College Press.

Dyson, A. H. (2013). The case of the missing childhoods: Methodological notes for composing children in writing studies. *Written Communication, 30*(4), 399–427. doi:10.1177/0741088313496383.

Edmiston, B. (2008). *Forming ethical identities in early childhood play: Contesting early childhood series*. New York, NY: Routledge.

Edwards, C. P., Gandini, L., & Forman, G. E. (1998). *The hundred languages of children: The Reggio Emilia approach-advanced reflections* (2nd ed.). Westport, CN: Ablex Publishing.

Edwards, S. (2013a). Digital play in the early years: A contextual response to the problem of integrating technologies and play-based pedagogies in the early childhood curriculum. *European Early Childhood Education Research Journal, 21*(2), 199–212.

Edwards, S. (2013b). Post-industrial play: Understanding the relationship between traditional and converged forms of play in the early years. In A. Burke & J. Marsh (Eds.), *Children's virtual worlds: Culture, learning and participation* (pp. 10–25). New York, NY: Peter Lang Publishing.

Ellis, J. (2004). Researching children's place and space. *Journal of Curriculum Theorizing, 20*(1), 83–99.

Evans, J. (2005). *Literacy moves on: Popular culture, new technologies, and critical literacy in the elementary classroom*. Portsmouth, NH: Heinemann.

Falloon, G. W. (2013a). What's going on behind the screens? Researching young students' learning pathways using iPads. *Journal of Computer-Assisted Learning, 30*(4), 318–336. doi:10.1111/jcal.12044.

Falloon, G. (2013b). Young students using iPads: App design and content influences on their learning pathways. *Computers & Education, 68*, 505–521.

Falloon, G. W., & Khoo, E. (2014). Exploring young peoples' talk in iPad-supported collaborative learning environments. *Computers & Education, 77*, 13–28.

Farman, J. (2015). Stories, spaces, and bodies: The production of embodied space through mobile media storytelling. *Communication Research and Practice*, 101–116. doi:10.1080/22041451.2015.1047941.

Fernández-López, Á., Rodríguez-Fórtiz, M. J., Rodríguez-Almendros, M. L., & Martínez-Segura, M. J. (2013). Mobile learning technology based on iOS devices to support students with special education needs. *Computers & Education, 61*, 77–90.

Fisher, B., Lucas, T., & Galstyan, A. (2013). The role of iPads in constructing collaborative learning spaces. *Technology, Knowledge and Learning, 18*, 165–178.

Flewitt, R. (2008). Multimodal literacies. In J. Marsh & E. Hallet (Eds.), *Desirable literacies: Approaches to language and literacy in the early years* (pp. 122–139). London, UK: Sage.

Flewitt, R. (2011). Bringing ethnography to a multimodal investigation of early literacy in a digital age. *Qualitative Research, 11*(3), 293–310.

Flewitt, R., Kucirkova, N., & Messer, D. (2014a). Touching the virtual, touching the real: iPads enabling literacy for students experiencing disability. *Australian Journal of Language and Literacy, 37*(2), 107–116.

Flewitt, R., Messer, D., & Kucirkova, N. (2014b). New directions for early literacy in a digital age: The iPad. *Journal of Early Childhood Literacy, 15*(3), 289–310. doi:10.1177/1468798414533560.

Friend, M., Cook, L., Hurley-Chamberlain, D., & Shamberger, C. (2010). Co-teaching: An illustration of the complexity of collaboration in special education. *Journal of Educational and Psychological Consultation, 20*(1), 9–27.

Frost, J. L. (2009). *A history of children's play and play environments: Toward a contemporary child-saving movement.* New York, NY: Routledge.

Fullan, M. (2013). *Stratosphere.* Toronto, ON: Pearson Canada.

Galarneau, L. L. (2005). Authentic learning experiences through play: Games, simulations and the construction of knowledge. *Simulations and the Construction of Knowledge.* Retrieved from www.digra.org/digital-library/

Garrett, J. T., Heller, K. W., Fowler, L. P., Alberto, P. A., Fredrick, L. D., & O'Rourke, C. M. (2011). Using speech recognition software to increase writing fluency for individuals with physical disabilities. *Journal of Special Education Technology, 19*(3), 5–14.

Gee, J. (2004). *Situated language and learning: A critique of traditional schooling.* New York, NY: Routledge.

Gee, J. P. (1996). *Social linguistics and literacies: Ideology in discourses* (2nd ed.). London, UK: Routledge Taylor & Francis Group.

Getting, S., & Swainey, K. (2012). First graders with iPads? *Learning & Leading with Technology, 40*(1), 24–27.

Gonzales, A. (2016). The contemporary US digital divide: From initial access to technology maintenance. *Information, Communication & Society, 19*(2), 234–248.

Gonzales, A. L. (2014). Health benefits and barriers to cell phone use in low-income U.S. neighborhoods: Indications of technology maintenance. *Mobile Media & Communication, 2,* 233–248.

Gonzales, A. L., Ems, L., & Suri, R. (2014). Cell phone disconnection disrupts access to healthcare and health resources: A technology maintenance perspective. *New Media & Society.* doi:10.1177/1461444814558670.

Goouch, K. (2008). Understanding playful pedagogies, play narratives and play spaces. *Early Years, 28*(1), 93–102.

Gray, L., Thomas, N., Lewis, L., & Tice, P. (2010). *Teachers' use of educational technology in US public schools, 2009: First look.* Washington, DC: National Center for Education Statistics, Institute of Education Sciences, US Department of Education.

Grimes, S. M., & Shade, L. R. (2005). Neopian economics of play: Children's cyberpets and online communities as immersive advertising in NeoPets.com. *International Journal of Media & Cultural Politics, 1*(2), 181–198.

Gutshall, T. L., & Kuby, C. R. (2013). Students as integral contributors to teacher research. *Talking Points, 25*(1), 2–8.

Haight, M., Quan-Haase, A., & Corbett, B. A. (2014). Revisiting the digital divide in Canada: The impact of demographic factors on access to the Internet, level of online activity, and social networking site usage. *Information, Communication & Society, 17*(4), 503–519. doi:10.1080/1369118X.2014.891633.

Harada, V. H., & Yoshina, J. M. (2004). Moving from rote to inquiry: Creating learning that counts. *Library Media Connection, 23*(2), 22–25.

Harwood, D. (2014). The digital world and the young child. *ChildLinks, 3,* 2–8.

Harwood, D. (2015). Crayons & iPads: Children's meaning making in a digital world. *An Leanbh Og (The Young Child) Journal, 9*(1), 107–120.

Harwood, D., Bajovic, M., Woloshyn, V., Di Cesare, D. M., Lane, L., & Scott, K. (2015). Intersecting spaces in early childhood education: Inquiry-based pedagogy and tablets. *The International Journal of Holistic Early Learning and Development, 1*(1), 53–67.

Hashey, A. (2014). Leveraging technology in self-regulated strategy development writing instruction: Improving persuasive wrting in adolescents with emotional and behavioral disorders. *Unpublished study.*

Hashey, A. I. (2015). A technology-enhanced approach to self-regulated strategy development: Engaging adolescents with emotional and behavioral disorders in argumentative writing (doctoral dissertation). University at Buffalo, Buffalo, NY.

Hatherly, A., & Chapman, B. (2013). Fostering motivation for literacy in early childhood education using iPads. *Computers In New Zealand Schools: Learning, Teaching, Technology, 25* (1–3), 138–151.

Hattie, J., & Timperley, H. (2007). The power of feedback. *Review of educational research, 77*(1), 81–112.

Haydon, T., MacSuga-Gage, A. S., Simonsen, B., & Hawkins, R. (2012). Opportunities to respond: A key component of effective instruction. *Beyond Behavior, 22*(1), 23–31.

Hayles, K. (2012). *How we think: Digital media and contemporary technogenesis.* Chicago, IL: University of Chicago Press.

Henderson, S., & Yeow, J. (2012, January). *iPad in education: A case study of iPad adoption and use in a primary school.* Paper presented at the 45th Hawaii International Conference on System Sciences, Honolulu, HI.

Hermans, R., Tondeur, J., van Braak, J., & Valcke, M. (2008). The impact of primary school teachers' educational beliefs on the classroom use of computers. *Computers & Education, 51,* 1499–1509.

Hlodan, O. (2010). Mobile learning anytime, anywhere. *BioScience, 60*(9), 682–682.

Holland, D., Lachicotte, W., Skinner, D., & Cain, C. (1998). *Identity and agency in cultural worlds.* Cambridge, MA: Harvard University Press.

Home Care Ontario. (2015). *Supporting Ontario's special needs strategy for children and youth.* Retrieved from www.homecareontario.ca/docs/default-source/position-papers/5-2a-special-needs-statement-march-2015.pdf?sfvrsn=4

Honeyford, M. (2013). The simultaneity of experience: Cultural identity, magical realism, and the artefactual in digital storytelling. *Literacy, 47*(1), 17–25.

Howe, N., & Strauss, W. (2000). *Millennials rising: The next great generation.* New York, NY: Vintage.

Hughes, P., & MacNaughton, G. (2000). Consensus, dissensus, or community: The politics of parent involvement in early childhood education. *Contemporary Issues in Early Childhood, 1*(3), 241–258.

Hultman, K., & Lenz Taguchi, H. (2010). Challenging anthropocentric analysis of visual data: A relational materialist methodological approach to educational research. *International Journal of Qualitative Studies in Education, 23*(5), 525–542.

Human Resources and Skills Development Canada. (2011). *Disability in Canada: A 2006 profile.* Ottawa, ON: Author. Retrieved from www.deslibris.ca/ID/228949

Hung, C., Sun, J. C., & Yu, P. (2015). The benefits of a challenge: Student motivation and flow experience in tablet-PC-game-based learning. *Interactive Learning Environments, 23*(2), 172–190.

Individuals with Disabilities Education Act, 20 U.S.C. § 1400 (2004).

Ito, M., Okabe, D., & Matsuda, M. (2006). *Personal, portable, pedestrian: Mobile phones in Japanese life.* Cambridge, MA: The MIT Press.

Januszewski, A. & Molenda, M., (2008). *Educational Technology: A Definition with Commentary.* London and New York: Routledge.

Jenkins, H. (2006). *Convergence culture: Where old and new media collide.* New York, NY: New York University Press.

Jenkins, H. (2009). *Confronting the challenges of participatory culture: Media education in the 21st century.* Cambridge, MA: MIT Press.

Jewitt, C., & Kress, G. (Eds.). (2003). *Multimodal literacy.* New York, NY: Peter Lang.

Johnson, E. S., Humphrey, M., Mellard, D. F., Woods, K., & Swanson, H. L. (2010). Cognitive processing deficits and students with specific learning disabilities: A selective meta-analysis of the literature. *Learning Disability Quarterly, 33*(1), 3–18.

Johnson, J. E., Christie, J. F., & Yawkey, T. D. (1999). *Play and early childhood development.* New York: Longman.

Kaczorowski, T. L. (2015). *eWorkbooks for mathematics: A mobile technology intervention designed to support students with and without disabilities during independent practice of whole number multiplication and division* (Doctoral dissertation). University at Buffalo, Buffalo, NY.

Kagohara, D. M., van der Meer, L., Ramdoss, S., O'Reilly, M. F., Lancioni, G. E., Davis, T. N., & Green, V. A. (2013). Using iPods® and iPads® in teaching programs for individuals with developmental disabilities: A systematic review. *Research in developmental disabilities, 34*(1), 147–156.

Kalantzis, M. (2006). Changing subjectivities, new learning. *Pedagogies, 1*(1), 7–12.

Kalliala, M. (2006). *Play culture in a changing world-Debating play series.* Maidenhead, UK: Open University Press.

Kay, K. (2010). 21st century skills: Why they matter, what they are, and how we get there. In J. Bellanca & R. Brandt (Eds.), *21st century skills: Rethinking how students learn* (pp. xiii–xxxi). Bloomington, IN: Solution Tree Press.

Kendrick, M. (2005). Playing house: A 'sideways' glance at literacy and identity in early childhood. *Journal of Early Childhood Literacy, 5*(1), 5–28.

Kervin, L., & Mantei, J. (2011). This is me: Children teaching us about themselves through digital storytelling. *Practically Primary, 16*(1), 4–7.

Kim, A. H., Vaughn, S., Wanzek, J., & Wei, S. (2004). Graphic organizers and their effects on the reading comprehension of students with LD-A synthesis of research. *Journal of Learning Disabilities, 37*(2), 105–118.

Kjallander, S., & Moinian, F. (2014). Digital tablets and applications in preschool–Preschoolers' creative transformation of didactic design. *Designs for Learning, 7*(1), 10–33.

Knobel, M., & Wilber, D. (2009). Let's talk 2.0. *Educational Leadership, 66*(6), 20–24.

Korat, O. (2010). Reading electronic books as a support for vocabulary, story comprehension and word reading in kindergarten and first grade. *Computers & Education, 55*(1), 24–31.

Korat, O., & Shamir, A. (2008). The educational electronic book as a scaffolding tool for children's emergent literacy in low versus middle SES groups. *Computers & Education, 50*, 110–124.

Korat, O., Levin, I., Ben-Shabt, A., Shneor, D., & Bokovza, L. (2014). Dynamic versus static dictionary with and without printed focal words in e-book reading as facilitator for word learning. *Reading Research Quarterly, 49*(4), 371–386.

Krechevsky, M. (2004). Form function and understanding in learning groups: Proposition from the Reggio classrooms. In C. Giudici, C. Rinaldi, & M. Krechevsky (Eds.), *Making learning visible: Children as individual and group learners* (pp. 78–81). Cambridge, MA: Project Zero and Reggio Children.

Kress, G. (1997). *Before writing: Rethinking the paths to literacy*, New York, NY: Routledge Press.

Kuby, C. R. (2013). *Critical literacy in the early childhood classroom: Unpacking histories, unlearning privilege*. New York, NY: Teachers College Press-Language and Literacy Series.

Kucirkova, N. (2014). iPads in early education: Separating assumptions and evidence. *Frontiers in Education, 5*, 1–3.

Kucirkova, N., Messer, D., Sheehy, K., & Panadero, C. F. (2014). Children's engagement with educational iPad apps: Insights from a Spanish classroom. *Computers & Education, 71*, 175–184.

Kultti, A., & Oldenbring, Y. (2015). Collective and individual dimensions in peer positioning in early childhood education, *Early Child Development and Care, 185* (6).

Labbo, L. D., & Kuhn, M. R. (2000). Weaving chains of affect and cognition: A young child's understanding of CD-ROM talking books. *Journal of Literacy Research, 32*(2), 187–210.

Labbo, L. D., & Reinking, D. (1999). Negotiating the multiple realities of technology in literacy research and instruction. *Reading Research Quarterly, 34*(4), 478–492.

Lackney, J. A. (2008). Teacher environmental competence in elementary school environments. *Children Youth and Environments, 18*(2), 133–159.

Lancaster, L. (2003). Beginning at the beginning: How a young child constructs time multimodally. In G. Kress & C. Jewitt (Eds.), *Multimodal literacy* (pp. 107–122), London, UK: Peter Lang.

Latour, B. (1992). *We have never been modern*. Cambridge, MA: Harvard University Press.

Leander, K. M., & Boldt, G. M. (2013). Rereading 'a pedagogy of multiliteracies': Bodies, texts, and emergence. *Journal of Literacy Research, 45*(1), 22–46.

Lensmire, T. (2000). *Powerful writing, responsible teaching*. New York, NY: Teachers College Press.

Lenz Taguchi, H. (2010). *Going beyond the theory/practice divide in early childhood education: Introducing the intra-active pedagogy*. London, UK: Routledge.

Levinas, E. (1989). Ethics as first philosophy. In S. Hand (Ed.), *The Levinas reader*. Oxford, UK: Blackwell Publishing.

Lim, S. S., & Clark, L. S. (2010). Virtual worlds as a site of convergence for children's play. *Journal for Virtual Worlds, 3*(2), 3–19.

Loris Malaguzzi International Centre. (2016). *Bordercrossings exhibit*. Reggio Emilia, Italy.

Luce-Kapler, R. (2006). Creative fragments: The subjunctive spaces of e-literature. *English Teaching: Practice and Critique, 5*(2), 6–16.

Lynch, J., & Redpath, T. (2014). 'Smart' technologies in early years literacy education: A metanarrative of paradigmatic tensions in iPad use in an Australian preparatory classroom. *Journal of Early Childhood Literacy, 14*(2), 147–174.

Male, T., & Burden, K. (2014). Access denied? Twenty-first-century technology in schools. *Technology, Pedagogy & Education, 23*(4), 423–437. doi:10.1080/14759 39X.2013.864697.

Maloch, B., & Horsey, M. (2013). Living inquiry: Learning from and about informational texts in a second-grade classroom. *Reading Teacher, 66*(6), 475–485.

Malone, T. W., & Lepper, M. R. (1987). Making learning fun: A taxonomy of intrinsic motivations for learning. In R. E. Snow & M. J. Farr (Eds.), *Aptitude, learning, and instruction: III. Conative and affective process analyses* (pp. 223–253). Hillsdale, NJ: Erlbaum.

Margaryan, A., Littlejohn, A., & Vojt, G. (2011). Are digital natives a myth or reality? University students' use of digital technologies. *Computers & Education, 56*, 429–440.

Marsh, J. (2004). The techno-literacy practices of young children. *Journal of Early Childhood Research, 2*(1), 51–66. doi:10.1177/1476718X0421003.

Marsh, J. (2010a). *Childhood, culture and creativity: A literature review.* Newcastle Upon Tyne, UK. Retrieved from www.creativitycultureeducation.org/wp-content/uploads/CCE-childhood-culture-and-creativity-a-literature-review.pdf

Marsh, J. (2010b). Young children's play in online virtual worlds. *Journal of Early Childhood Research, 8*(1), 23–39.

Marsh, J. (2014). Media, popular culture and play. In L. Brooker, M. Blaise, & S. Edwards (Eds.), *The Sage handbook of play and learning in early childhood* (pp. 403–414). London, UK: Sage.

Marsh, J. (2011). Young children's literacy practices in a virtual world: Establishing an online interaction order. *Reading Research Quarterly, 46*(2), 101–118.

Marsh, J., & Bishop, J. C. (2014). *Changing play: Play, media and commercial culture from the 1950's to the present day.* Maidenhead, UK: Open University Press.

Mascheroni, G., & Ólafsson, K. (2014). *Net children go mobile: Cross-national comparisons* (No. Report D3.3). Milan, Italy: Educatt.

Mayfield, M. (2001). *Early childhood education and care in Canada: Contexts, dimensions, and issues.* Toronto, ON: Prentice Hall.

McClanahan, B., Williams, K., Kennedy, E., & Tate, S. (2012). A breakthrough for Josh: How use of an iPad facilitated reading improvement. *TechTrends, 56*(3), 20–28.

McLuhan, M. (1964). *Understanding media: The extensions of man.* Cambridge, MA: MIT press.

McManis, L. D., & Gunnewig, S. B. (2012). Finding the education in educational technology with early learners. *Young Children, 67*(3), 14–24. doi:10.1111/j.1467-8535.2012.01323.x.

McPake, J., Plowman, L., & Stephen, C. (2013). Pre-school children creating and communicating with digital technologies in the home. *British Journal of Educational Technology, 44*(3), 421–431.

McTavish, M. (2014). 'I'll do it my own way!' A young child's appropriation and recontextualization of school literacy practices in out-of-school spaces. *Journal of Early Childhood Literacy, 14*(3), 319–344.

MediaSmarts. (2014). *Young Canadians in a wired world, phase III: Life online.* Retrieved from http://mediasmarts.ca/ycww/life-online

Melhuish, K., & Falloon, G. (2010). Looking to the future: M-learning with the iPad. *Computers in New Zealand Schools: Learning, Leading, Technology, 22*(30), 1–15.

Meyer, A., Rose, D. H., & Gordon, D. (2014). *Universal design for learning: Theory and practice.* Wakefield, MA: CAST.

Miller, B. T., Krockover, G. H., & Doughty, T. (2013). Using iPads to teach science to students with a moderate to severe intellectual disability: A pilot study. *Journal of Research in Science Teaching, 50*(8), 887–911.

Moses, L. (2012). *Data points: Wired child preschoolers have more exposure to electronics than ever.* Retrieved from www.adweek.com/news/technology/data-points-wired-child-143732

Moss, P. (2014). *Early childhood and compulsory education: Reconceptualising the relationship.* New York, NY: Routledge.

Muis, K. R., Ranellucci, J., Trevors, G., & Duffy, M. C. (2015). The effects of technology-mediated immediate feedback on kindergarten children' attitudes, emotions, engagement, and learning outcomes during literacy skills development. *Learning and Instruction, 38,* 1–13.

Neslihan Bay, D. (2015). Examining the participation of preschool children in the writing center during free choice times. *Reading Improvement, 52*(1), 9–18.

Neumann, M. M., & Neumann, D. L. (2014). Touch screen tablets and emergent literacy. *Early Childhood Education Journal, 42*(4), 231–239.

Neumann, S. (2014). An examination of touch screen tablets and emergent literacy in Australian pre-school children. *Australian Journal of Education, 58*(2), 109–122. doi:10.1177/0004944114523368.

Neumann, S., Copple, C., & Bredekamp, S. (2000). *Learning to read and write: Developmentally appropriate practices for young children.* Washington, DC: National Association for the Education of Young Children.

New London Group. (2000). A pedagogy of multiliteracies: Designing social futures. In B. Cope & M. Kalanzis (Eds.), *Multiliteracies: Literacy learning and the design of social futures* (pp. 9–37). New York, NY: Routledge.

Noce, A. A., & McKeown, L. (2008). A new benchmark for Internet use: A logistic modeling of factors influencing Internet use in Canada, 2005. *Government Information Quarterly, 25,* 462–476. doi:10.1016/j.giq.2007.04.006.

Nolen, S. B. (2007). Young children's motivation to read and write: Development in social contexts. *Cognition & Instruction, 25*(2/3), 219–270.

O'Brien, D., & Scharber, C. (2006). Digital literacies go to school: Potholes and possibilities. *Journal of Adolescent and Adult Literacy, 52*(1), 66–68.

Ofcom. (2013). *Children and parents: Media use and attitudes report.* Retrieved from http://stakeholders.ofcom.org.uk/market-data-research/other/research-publications/childrens/children-parents-oct-2013/

Olsson, L. M. (2009). *Movement and experimentation in young children's learning: Deleuze and Guattari in early childhood educations.* New York, NY: Routledge.

O'Mara, J., & Laidlaw, L. (2011). Living in the iworld: Two literacy researchers reflect on the changing texts and literacy practices of childhood. *English Teaching: Practice and Critique, 10*(4), 149–159.

Ontario Ministry of Education. (2015). *The kindergarten program.* Toronto, ON: Queen's Printer for Ontario.

Ontario Ministry of Education. (2014). *How does learning happen? Ontario's pedagogy for the early years.* Toronto, ON: Queen's Printer for Ontario.

Pacini-Ketchabaw, V., Nxumalo, F., Kocher, L., Elliot, E., & Sanchez, A. (2015). *Journeys: Reconceptualizing early childhood through pedagogical narration.* Toronto, ON: Toronto University Press.

Pahl, K., & Rowsell, J. (Eds.). (2006). *Travel notes from the new literacy studies: Instances of practice.* Clevedon, UK: Multilingual Matters.

Partnership for 21st Century Learning (2015). *The 4Cs research series.* Retrieved from www.p21.org/our-work/4cs-research-series

Pelo, A. (2006). Growing a culture of inquiry: Observation as professional development. *Exchange, The Early Readers' Magazine, 172,* 50–53.

Penuel, W. R. (2006). Implementation and effects of one-to-one computing initiatives: A research synthesis. *Journal of research on technology in education, 38*(3), 329–348.

Perez, L. (2013). *Mobile learning for all: Supporting accessibility with the iPad.* Thousand Oaks, CA: Corwin.

Piaget, J. (2001). *The psychology of intelligence.* London, UK: Routledge.

Piaget, J. (2007). *The child's conception of the world.* Lanham, MD: Rowman & Littlefield.

Phillips, B., & Zhao, H. (1993). Predictors of assistive technology abandonment. *Assistive Technology, 5*(1), 36–45.

Plowman, L., & McPake, J. (2013). Seven myths about young children and technology. *Childhood Education, 89*(1), 27–33.

Plowman, L., McPake, J., & Stephen, C. (2008). Just picking it up? Young children learning with technology at home. *Cambridge Journal of Education, 38*(3), 303–319.

Plowman, L., McPake, J., & Stephen, C. (2010). The technologisation of childhood? Young children and technology in the home. *Children & Society, 24*(1), 63–74.

Plowman, L., & Stevenson, O. (2012). Using mobile phone diaries to explore children's everyday lives. *Childhood: A Global Journal of Child Research, 19*(4), 539–553.

Plowman, L., Stevenson, O., Stephen, C., & McPake, J. (2012). Preschool children's learning with technology at home. *Computers & Education, 59*(1), 30–37.

Prensky, M. (2001). Digital natives, digital immigrants Part 1. *On the Horizon, 9*(5), 1.

Price, S., & Rogers, Y. (2004). Let's get physical: The learning benefits of interacting in digitally augmented physical spaces. *Computers & Education, 43*(1), 137–151.

Prinsloo, M. (2005). The new literacies as placed resources. *Perspectives in Education, 23*(4), 87–98.

Prinsloo, M., & Rowsell, J. (2012). Introduction: Digital literacies as placed resources in the globalised periphery. *Language and Education, 26*(4), 271–277.

Radich, J. (2013). Technology and interactive media as tools in early childhood programs serving children from birth through age 8. *Every Child, 19*(4), 18–19.

Ragnedda, M., & Muschert, G. W. (2013). *The digital divide: The internet and social inequality in international perspective.* New York, NY: Routledge.

Rasmussen, K. (2004). Places for children–children's places. *Childhood, 11*(2), 155–173.

Reiser, B. J. (2004). Scaffolding complex learning: The mechanisms of structuring and problematizing student work. *The Journal of the Learning Sciences, 13*(3), 273–304.

Rideout, V. J., Vandewater, E. A., & Wartella, E. A. (2003). *Zero to six: Electronic media in the lives of infants, toddlers, and preschoolers.* Menlo Park, CA: Henry J. Kaiser Family Foundation. Retrieved from www.kff.org/entmedia/3378.cfm

Rinaldi, C. (2004). Documentation and assessment: What is the relationship? In C. Guidici, C. Rinaldi, & M. Krechevsky (Eds.), *Making learning visible: Children as individual and group learners* (pp. 78–89). Cambridge, MA: Project Zero and Reggio Children.

Rinaldi, C. (2006). *In dialogue with Reggio Emilia: Listening, researching, and learning.* New York, NY: Routledge.

Rogers, V., & Whittaker, L. (2010). Keeping kids keen: Being influenced by the Reggio Emilia philosophy in a P-1 classroom. *Educating Young Children, 16*(2), 39–41.

Rose, D. H., Hasselbring, T. S., Stahl, S., & Zabala, J. (2005). Assistive technology and universal design for learning: Two sides of the same coin. *Handbook of special education technology research and practice, 507–518.*

Rose, D. H., & Meyer, A. (2002). *Teaching every student in the digital age: Universal design for learning.* Alexandria, VA: Association for Supervision and Curriculum Development.

Rose, K. K., Vittrup, B., & Leveridge, T. (2013). Parental decision-making about technology and quality in child care programs. *Child & Youth Care Forum, 42*(5), 475–488. doi:10.1007/s10566-013-9214-1.

Rose, S. (2012). *Putting narrative documentation to work: A search for educational abundance.* Unpublished doctoral dissertation, Fredericton, NB: University New Brunswick.

Rowe, F. A., & Rafferty, J. A. (2013). Instructional design interventions for supporting self-regulated learning: enhancing academic outcomes in postsecondary e-learning environments. *Journal of Online Learning and Teaching, 9*(4), 590–601.

Rowsell, J., Colquhoun, C., & Maues, F. (in press). Apps and autodidacts: Capturing reading processes and practices on iPads. In C. Burnett, G. Merchant, A. Simpson, & M. Walsh (Eds.), *Mobile literacies and iPad pedagogies.* New York, NY: Peter Lang.

Rowsell, J., & Gallagher, T. (in press). Circuits, astronauts, and dancing oranges: Documenting networked knowledge on iPads. In S. Nichols & M. de Courcy (Eds.), *Languages and literacies as mobile and placed resources* (pp. 45–60). London, UK: Routledge.

Rowsell, J., & Harwood, D. (2015). 'Let it go': Exploring the image of the child as a producer, consumer, and inventor. *Theory into Practice Journal-Special Edition, 54*(2), 136–146. doi:10.1080/00405841.2015.1010847.

Rowsell, J., & Wohlwend, K. E. (2016). Free play or tight spaces? Mapping participatory literacies in apps. *The Reading Teacher, 70*(2), 197–205. doi:10.1002/trtr.1490.

Schwartzman, H. (1976). Children's play: A sideways glance at make-believe. In D. F. Lancy & B. A. Tindall (Eds.), *The study of play: Problems and prospects* (pp. 208–215). New York, NY: Leisure Press.

Selouani, S., & Hamam, H. (2007). Social impact of broadband Internet: A case study in the Shippagan area, a rural zone in Atlantic Canada. *Journal of Information, Information Technology & Organizations, 279–294.*

Selwyn, N. (2004). Reconsidering political and popular understandings of the digital divide. *New Media & Society, 6*(3), 341–362. doi:10.1177/1461444804042519.

Selwyn, N., & Facer, K. (2014). The sociology of education and digital technology: Past, present and future. *Oxford Review of Education, 40*(4), 482. doi:10.1080/03054985.2014.933005.

Selwyn, N., Potter, J., & Cranmer, S. (2009). Primary pupils' use of information and communication technologies at school and home. *British Journal of Educational Technology, 40*(5), 919–932.

Seo, Y. J., & Bryant, D. P. (2009). Analysis of studies of the effects of computer-assisted instruction on the mathematics performance of students with learning disabilities. *Computers & Education, 53*(3), 913–928.

Silió, M. C., & Barbetta, P. M. (2010). The effects of word prediction and text-to-speech technologies on the narrative writing skills of Hispanic students with specific learning disabilities. *Journal of Special Education Technology, 25*(4), 17.

Singer, D. G., & Singer, J. L. (2005). *Imagination and play in the electronic age.* Cambridge, MA: Harvard University Press.

Singh, S. (2010). Independent and collaborative writing in a kindergarten classroom. *Journal of Reading Education, 36*(1), 48–53.

Snow, C. E., Burns, M. S., & Griffin, P. (Eds.). (1998). *Preventing reading difficulties in young children.* Washington, DC: National Academy Press.

Sørensen, B. H., Danielsen, O., & Nielsen, J. (2007). Children's informal learning in the context of schools of the knowledge society. *Education Information Technology, 12*(1), 17–27. doi:10.1007/s10639-006-9019-z.

Statista. (2016a). *Number of available apps in the apple app store.* Retrieved from www.statista.com/statistics/263795/number-of-available-apps-in-the-apple-app-store/

Statista. (2016b). *Most popular apple app store categories in March 2016, by share of available apps.* Retrieved from www.statista.com/statistics/270291/popular-categories-in-the-app-store/

Stein, P. (2008). *Multimodal pedagogies in diverse classrooms: Representation, rights, and resources.* London, UK: Routledge.

Stephen, C., & Plowman, L. (2014). Digital play. In L. Booker, M. Blaise & S. Edward (Eds.), *The Sage book of play and learning in early childhood.* London, UK: Sage.

Stephen, C., Stevenson, O., & Adey, C. (2013). Young children engaging with technologies at home: The influence of family context. *Journal of Early Childhood Research, 11*(2), 149.

Strong-Wilson, T., & Ellis, J. (2007). Children and place: Reggio Emilia's environment as third teacher. *Theory into Practice, 46*(1), 40–47.

Sutherland, K. S., Alder, N., & Gunter, P. L. (2003). The effect of varying rates of opportunities to respond to academic requests on the classroom behavior of students with EBD. *Journal of Emotional and Behavioral Disorders, 11*(4), 239–248.

Sutton-Smith, B. (1997). *The ambiguity of play.* Cambridge, MA: Harvard University Press.

Tahnk, J. L. (2011). Digital milestones: Raising a tech-savvy kid. *Parenting Early Years, 25,* 78–84.

Tarr, P. (2004). *Consider the walls.* Retrieved from http://oldweb.naeyc.org/journal/btj/200405/walls.asp

Taylor, A., Pacini-Ketchabaw, V., & Blaise, M. (Eds.). (2012). Children's relations with the more-than-human world. *Contemporary Issues in Early Childhood, 13*(2). Retrieved from http://cie.sagepub.com/content/13/2/81

Taylor, A. (2013). *Reconfiguring the natures of childhood.* New York, NY: Routledge.

Thiel, J. J. (2015). 'Bumblebee's in trouble!': Embodied literacies during imaginative superhero play. *Language Arts, 93*(1), 38–49.

Tonn, J. (2013). A foray into the iPad world. *Early Childhood Education, 41*(1), 19–24.

Troia, G. A. (2006). Writing instruction for students with learning disabilities. In C. MacArthur, S. Graham, & J. Fitzgerald (Eds.), *Handbook of writing research* (pp. 324–326). New York, NY: Guilford Press.

Turkle, S. (Ed.). (2007). *Evocative objects: Things we think with.* Massachusetts, MA: MIT Press.

UNESCO. (2006). Understandings of literacy. *Education for All Global Monitoring Report.* Retrieved from www.unesco.org/education/GMR2006/full/chapt6_eng.pdf

U.S. Department of Education. (2014). *36th annual report to congress on the implementation of the Individuals with Disabilities Education Act, Parts B. and C. 2014.* Washington, DC: U.S. Department of Education, Office of Special Education and Rehabilitative Services, Office of Special Education Programs.

van Dijk, J. A. G. M. (2006). Digital divide research, achievements, and shortcomings. *Poetics, 34*, 221–235.

Vandewater, E. A., Rideout, V. J., Wartella,E. A., Xuan Huang, Lee, J. H. & Shim, M. (2007). Digital childhood: electronic media and technology use among infants, toddlers, and preschoolers. http://pediatrics.aappublications.org/content/119/5/e1006..info

Vangsnes, V., Okland, N. T. G., & Krumsvik, R. (2012). Computer games in pre-school settings: Didactical challenges when commercial educational computer games are implemented in kindergartens. *Computers & Education, 58*(4), 1138–1148. doi:10.1016/j.compedu.2011.12.018.

Vasquez, V. M., & Felderman, C. B. (2013). *Technology and critical literacy in early childhood.* New York, NY: Routledge.

Vasudevan, L., Schultz, K., & Bateman, J. (2010). Rethinking composing in a digital age: Authoring literate identities through multimodal storytelling. *Written Communication, 27*(4), 442–468.

Vogel, D., Kennedy, D. M., & Kwok, R. (2009). Does using mobile device applications lead to learning? *Journal of Interactive Learning Research, 20*, 469–485.

Vratulis, V., & Winters, K. L. (2013). Puppets don't have legs! Dinosaurs have digits! Using the dramatic and media arts to deepen knowledge across content areas. *Education Matters, 1*(2), 91–110.

Vygotsky, L. (1962). *Thought and language.* (E. Hanfmann & G. Vakar, Trans.). Cambridge, MA: MIT Press.

Walker, H. (2011). Evaluating the effectiveness of apps for mobile devices. *Journal of Special Education Technology, 26*(4): 59–63.

Wang, F., Kinzie, M., McGuire, P., & Pan, E. (2010). Applying technology to inquiry-based learning in early childhood education. *Early Childhood Education Journal, 37*(5), 381–389.

Wein, C. A., Coates, A., Keating, B. L., & Bigelow, B. C. (2005). *Designing the environment to build connection to place.* Retrieved from www.naeyc.org/files/yc/file/200505/05wein.pdf

Wein, C. A. (2008). *Emergent curriculum in the primary classroom.* New York, NY: Teachers College Press.

Wells, C. G. (1999). *Dialogic inquiry: Towards a sociocultural practice and theory of education.* New York, NY: Cambridge University Press.

What Works Clearinghouse. (2011). *Peer assisted learning strategies* (WWC Intervention Report). Retrieved from http://ies.ed.gov/ncee/wwc/pdf/intervention_reports/wwc_pals_060512.pdf

Winters, K., McLauchlan, D., & Fournier. (2015). 'You do this and I'll do that': Co-authorship, authority, and playbuilding in a Canadian community based project for impoverished youth. In M. Carter, M. Prendergast, & G. Belliveau (Eds.), *Drama, theatre and performance education in Canada: Classroom and community contexts* (pp. 74–85). Ottawa, ON: Canadian Association for Teacher Education Polygraph Series.

Winters, K., & Vratulis, V. (2012). Authored assemblages in a digital world: Illustrations of a child's online, social, critical, and semiotic meaning making. *Journal of Early Childhood Literacy, 13*(4), 529–554.

Wohlwend, K. E. (2010). A is for avatar: Young children in literacy 2.0 worlds and literacy 1.0 schools. *Language Arts, 88*, 144–152.

Wohlwend, K. E. (2011). *Playing their way into literacies: Reading, writing, and belonging in the early childhood classroom.* New York, NY: Teachers College Press.

Wohlwend, K. E. (2013). *Literacy playshop: New literacies, popular media, and play in the early childhood classroom.* New York, NY: Teachers College Press.

Wohlwend, K. E. (2014). Making, remaking, and reimagining the everyday: Play, creativity and popular media. In J. Rowsell & K. Pahl (Eds.), *The routledge handbook of literacy studies* (pp. 548–560). London, UK: Routledge.

Wohlwend, K., Medina, C. L. (2014). Producing cultural imaginaries in the playshop. In R. Meyer & K. Whitmore (Eds.), *Reclaiming writing: Composing spaces for identities, relationships and action* (pp. 198–209). New York, NY: Routledge.

Wohlwend, K. E., & Merchant, G. (2013). Learning, literacies and new technologies: The current context and future possibilities. In J. Larson & J. Marsh (Eds.), *The SAGE handbook of early childhood literacy* (pp. 575–587). London, UK: Sage.

Wong, S. S. (2015). Mobile digital devices and preschoolers' home multiliteracy practices. *Language and Literacy, 17*(2), 75–90.

Wu, W. H., Wu, Y. C. J., Chen, C. Y., Kao, H. Y., Lin, C. H., & Huang, S. H. (2012). Review of trends from mobile learning studies: A meta-analysis. *Computers & Education, 59*(2), 817–827.

Yelland, N. (2011). Reconceptualising play and learning in the lives of young children. *Australasian Journal of Early Childhood, 36*(2), 4–12.

Yelland, N., Lee, L., O'Rourke, M., & Harrison, C. (2008). *Rethinking learning in early childhood education.* Berkshire, UK: Open University Press.

Zevenbergen, R. (2007). Digital natives come to preschool: Implications for early childhood practice. *Contemporary Issues in Early Childhood, 8*(1), 19–29.

Zigmond, N., Kloo, A., & Volonino, V. (2009). What, where, and how? Special education in the climate of full inclusion. *Exceptionality, 17*(4), 189–204.

Zosh, J. M., Hirsh-Pasek, K., Golinkoff, R. M., & Parish-Morris, J. (2016). Learning in the digital age: Putting education back in educational apps for young children. *Encyclopedia on early childhood development.* Retrieved from www.child-encyclopedia.com/sites/default/files/textes-experts/en/4738/learning-in-the-digital-age-putting-education-back-in-educational-apps-for-young-children.pdf

INDEX